The Charity Letters of

JoAnn Cayce

Compiled and Edited

by

Marcia Camp

Library of Congress Control Number: 2007941718
ISBN   978-0-9801231-0-4

Photo credits:
JoAnn Cayce photo courtesy of *Caring People*
Marcia Camp photo by Angela Camp Dyke

Book Design by Allen Lee, Nimbus Books

1st Edition
January 2008

Bright Cloud Press
5128 B Street
Little Rock, Arkansas 72205

Table of Contents

Dedication

I would like to dedicate this book to my dear husband and my four children, Joannie, Kandy, Paul, and Gaye, who have always, since they learned to talk, been my supporters, also grandchildren Cayce, Daniel, Audrey, and Whitney. My husband has helped in everything I have ever done for the poor and people in trouble if I needed him. Hartsel offered advice many times when I did not know which way to turn. He has gone with me in dangerous situations and encouraged me when I became so low I would have stopped without him. My dear mother, Jewel James, helped the poor all my growing years, and she showed by her example what true charity and giving of oneself really meant. All these dear people are true examples of caring for your fellow man.

Foreword

I first spoke with JoAnn Cayce in late 1997. She had just won the Sister Pierre Voster Outstanding Volunteer Award, and the editor of *Aging Arkansas* asked me to write a profile about her. The telephone interview was set for 7:30 in the morning, before JoAnn's day became too busy, and she began to recite some of her day-to-day experiences with the poor.

Taking notes at my desk, I fought back tears and tried to keep control of my voice so that I could continue the interview in a professional manner. I realized immediately that this was a very special lady.

After publication of the profile and an essay for the *Arkansas Democrat Gazette*, I kept in touch with JoAnn, driving to Thornton with a carload of men's trousers salvaged from a warehouse fire. She put me on her Charity Letters mailing list, and I learned even more about her remarkable work.

Early on, I decided that the plight of the rural poor needed to be documented and thought that film was the only medium that could be believed. I wanted to make a short documentary built around an interview with JoAnn but including comments from doctors, social workers, and persons who implement government programs in order to show the impossible situations of the poverty stricken, but I had no money.

When JoAnn began to have "little strokes" in early 2003, I knew that money or not, I had to get her on tape because she was the only person who could tell this story. I found the perfect filmmaker, Sandra Hubbard, sold her on the idea, and we began taping interviews and food and clothing give-aways, using my "butter and egg money."

Years ago, the only discretionary income a woman had was what she collected from selling the butter she made or the eggs she gathered. For me, it meant every penny I could spare.

During the visits to Thornton, where the film was being shot, JoAnn often mentioned her desire to write a book, an effort we both recognized as a pipe-dream. She was too busy actually caring for the poor to write about them. In early 2005, I woke up in the middle of the night with the realization that JoAnn had already written her book without realizing it—everything was perfectly recorded in her Charity Letters.

I made arrangements with her to publish the letters I had collected since we first met and those few that she had saved over the years. (Most of the letters are undated, and I have tried to establish a time-line.) They remain unedited and unabridged so as to retain JoAnn's voice—the voice of authenticity that none other than her own words convey. Only an occasional last name of someone she has helped has been deleted to protect their privacy.

I might add at this point that I chose to make the film in Thornton and other locations in Arkansas because this is where I "found" the story, not because this is a unique location for poverty (though rural poverty is extreme). With limited resources, I needed to be able to interview those persons who were dealing with this particular type of poverty and who were serving some of the same clients as JoAnn was seeing daily.

This Foreword and the Conclusion describing Daniel Cayce's work and awards are my writing. The Introduction and Dedication are JoAnn's words, written years ago as the beginning of her envisioned book.

The following pages are a chronicle of suffering and poverty, but they are also a tribute to the courage and dedication of JoAnn's family in the face of almost insurmountable odds, physical and emotional as well as financial.

Daily miracles (recognized and accepted as such) have allowed JoAnn to keep her charity going while Joannie's strong, quiet presence has sustained and linked that work with the future, Daniel.

In illuminating the plight of the poor through day-to-day

observations, JoAnn has also illustrated the failure of various programs designed to help them. Both sides of the coin are equally telling.

I am but the "mid-wife" in the birthing of this book filled with information too important to be ignored and too heart-wrenching to go unanswered.

All proceeds go to JoAnn Cayce Charities.

Marcia Camp

As it is, though, I'll do what little I can in writing. Only it will be very little. I'm not capable of it; and if I were, you would not go near it at all. For if you did, you would hardly bear to live.

—James Agee
Let Us Now Praise Famous Men

Introduction

My name is JoAnn Cayce. I was born in 1932, in the middle of the Depression, and I started helping people by driving my mother, Jewel, who did not drive.

If you are looking for a big literary work, this is not the book. I have never written any books before, and I just did not want to die without people having known what we have experienced working with the poor for a lifetime. There have been things I have seen that no human has ever seen or experienced in the South or in the United States. I thought these things should go on record. If you grow and get charity or better understand the things poor people endure without education or money or jobs, my life has not been in vain. I pray you wake up if you have slept through your blessings of life and never knew you were blessed beyond description. To not have toilet paper, a dime for the pay telephone across the street, or medicine money for a life-threatening illness, or break a leg and no way to get a doctor to see you and the hospital will not take you without insurance is trouble. I have seen it all my life. I would like to tell you about it.

Although it was my mother's example that set me on the path, it was her mother who showed her the way. My grandmother nursed people during the flu epidemic in 1918, and this started her life of service. She lost five of her eight children trying to care for them and help people. There was no money after her husband ran off with a lady from the bakery he owned. It was mortgaged to the hilt as was the house, which they lost. She tried to make the winter in a smoke house and use turnip greens she had canned and black berries she would pick. There was no money, then the flu hit. She lived to 103 with my mother.

It was Mother who performed the first act of charity that I remember when I must have been about four. I have never forgotten it. My eyes still mist, and I can still see the man sitting on the wooden box that held ice in my father's old country store. This must have been about 1936, and during the Depression. This man had maybe six children and no job. He was too sick to work if he had been able to find a job. He had T.B. He coughed all the time, but my mother did not run from him, or if I remember right, fail to give him the things she could get her hands on to help him. My grandfather, Dr. D.E. James, was the old country doctor who waited on everyone. My mother, his daughter-in-law, was his nurse, besides helping my father, Gurt James, run a country store. I remember my mother was someone everyone loved and her goodness and interest in humanity was well known.

This man was so sick, and I remember my mother asking that hot day if there was anything she could do for him. He said no. My mother asked him if there was anything he felt he could eat. He was skin and bones, and his skin color was like chalk. I still can see his face. Mr. Smith (not his real name) said, "I have craved celery, and I would love to have a stalk of celery. I think I could eat the whole stalk." Of course we were in a very small town with three businesses in 1936, and there were no celery or green vegetables unless you were able to have a garden, which he wasn't. My dear mother had no transportation, and the nearest place she could buy celery was in Camden, Arkansas. My parents sold cigarettes, and the salesman who sold them lived in Camden. My mother asked him that day to bring her a stalk of celery when he came back that week.

She gave him the money to buy a stalk, and he brought it back. Mr. Smith was still living and coughing but not able to come to town. I remember us walking down the dusty hill and my mother carrying Mr. Smith a stalk of clean celery. She had drawn a bucket of well water and washed it and got my brother and I cleaned up to go for the visit. Mr. Smith cried when he saw all of us and the celery. I will never forget him eating the stalk in front of us with salt. In a few days we heard he had passed away with consumption. They put that label on everything in those days. He was buried in a pine box with a closed lid and the whole community turned out, and my mother never said anything about her deed. No one would have been surprised because my mother was always going above and beyond.

This, as far as I remember, was the first charity act by my mother I remember. I have never discussed it with my brother who is 14 months older than I and who has always gone out of his way for others.

The second act, I remember seeing my mother do (and that day I realized she was unusual) made another lasting impression on my memory. I must have been about eight or nine. We had moved to Thornton, Arkansas. My father had another country store because our old store in Holly Springs had burned, and since we lived in the back, we had no business or home. Thornton was maybe 25 miles from Holly Springs where my brother and I had been born. One thing that was different about the new business was there was a bus station in the store. They also sold beer, wine, and sandwiches as well as groceries, and the Second World War was close on us. One day a man I remember as being very poor and without transportation came with tears telling my mother about his little girl who had stepped in hot coals around a wash pot while her mother was washing. He had talked to Dr. T.E. Rhine, another old country doctor who later we grew to love and wonder what the country would do without him. My own grandfather, the doctor, had died.

Dr. Rhine had advised them to get the child to Children's Hospital in Little Rock, 80 miles away. They had no way, and someone had told him that if anyone would make a way for his child to have skin grafts and treatment, Mrs. Jewel James would. Of course they had no insurance or money and probably had never been out of town much less to Little Rock. My mother told him to get the child ready and bring her the next day at a certain time, and she would put them on the Greyhound bus and send them to Little Rock. I remember my mother worrying and worrying about getting the driver to take the child and how would she get her to Children's after she got her to Little Rock. The next day, the parents came dressed in common clothes with the little girl wrapped in a clean sheet over her burned legs and feet and crying in pain. They sat outside on the old bench as there was no place to sit inside. Mother waited outside with them. The customers just had to wait or let my brother try to wait on them. Mother had fixed a ticket for all the family and paid for it herself.

Money was, of course, very hard in those days, but Mother never thought about that, she just thought about getting the job done. When the bus pulled up, they all went to the bus, my mother first in line. I don't suppose the family had ever ridden a bus before, and I am sure now they were scared to death. They had to have been tired because they had both walked at least five miles and carried the child.

Mother got on the bus with the tickets and what she told the bus driver I wish I knew, but when she came down and stepped out she said for them to get on and the bus driver was going to take them by Children's Hospital, and she would call ahead and tell them she would arrive. I remember my sweet mother coming into the store crying and going to the phone. The phone in those days was different—you had a wind-up receiver, and the operator came on and said "number please." My mother made the arrangements not only for the child to have surgery but for the parents a place to sleep, eat, and for the bill to be completely paid. She said call her when they were ready to come home and she would make a way for that. She gave the number for the store and her name.

I saw this family many times after that because if they had a dime, they spent it with my parents. I never saw them without thinking that child had normal feet and was able to walk on scarred legs because my mother cared enough to go out of her way to step out on faith and make a way where there was no way.

After the burn case, Dr. Rhine was my mother's best friend. He came to the store often and sent her many people who needed help. My brother or I took notes back and forth to Dr. Rhine's office because Mother did not want to tie up his line on the old phone.

The third and last incident I will tell you about concerning my mother is one I remember when I was maybe ten years old. We were in the middle of World War II, and no white person wanted to be seen or heard of helping a black person. My mother and Dr. Rhine paid no attention to color. They loved everyone and would help anyone. Doctor came one morning for gas, he would not come in because my family sold beer and wine and was known for running a rough place. My mother or my brother or I would run out to wait on Dr. Rhine when he came up to get gas every morning. If I remember gas was 18¢ a gallon in those days, and the pumps were just what I said, "pumps." My brother and I loved to pump gas in Dr. Rhine's car. That was in comparison to waiting on Jesus to a child. He was so important and always in a hurry.

The morning I have in mind, Dr. Rhine asked me to go get my mother. I went in quickly while my brother put the gas in, and Mother hurried out when she found it was Dr. Rhine who wanted to see her. He told her of a black lady who needed her badly. He told her to carry clean rags and go quickly to a certain house up in the quarters. He said he had a farm accident to hurry to, and he had to leave her, but he was sure the lady was miscarrying, bleeding badly. I did not know what that meant, but I ran in and went to the rag box and began to put clean rags in a grocery bag. When Mother came in, she told me I could not go with her. By then my father had an old A Model car, and the man who fixed flats would drive my mother up in the quarters and stay with her for safety purposes. Of course, no one would hurt my mother no more than they would hurt Dr. Rhine. At the last minute they were ready to leave, I jumped in the back of the A Model. My mother was in such a hurry, she did not argue. I guess she thought I could play with all the other kids while she worked. We went in, and the lady was screaming. I remember the coal oil light and the wood fire. I remember the hound dog lying on the floor and all that bunch of kids. I remember wishing I had brought them a bag of all-day suckers.

I don't know what my mother did, but she had the man draw a bucket of water, and she was there a long time. We played marbles, and I showed them my bean shooter. I did not know girl's games because I had a brother, and he had boys for friends, and I did not know any girls. Finally, Mother gave instructions and we left, and Mother woke the driver, and he cranked the A Model as the children watched. I remember feeling like a queen as they watched, and we drove off down the muddy and rough road. I am sure Mother went back to check on the lady later, but I do not remember that.

Those three things and more are my examples of what I wanted to do in life. I wanted to go where I was needed and carry a bag of supplies to people who would love me and appreciate me. That all came to pass in due time and that is what this book is all about.

* * *

I married Hartsel Cayce in 1947, and in a few years the babies came, three in four years. I started saving everything they had to give away to someone who needed the same. You call it recycling these days. In those days they called it "sharing." I would put the three children in our old pick-up and start out. I didn't have any food, but I took everything I could gather. I went to the poor areas and sat the babies out first and then the boxes. The families would see the truck and come and start looking. It was first come, first served. When the truck was empty, we went home. Sometimes a mother would tell me about a need she had, and I would look for it. I would watch for trash by the roadside, and if there was anything I could give to someone. First thing you know, people started setting things on our porch. Then a lady came to see us and attended a church meeting at our church. She saw what I was trying to do, and she started mailing me boxes from Chicago. This was the beginning of outside help. She got others to help, and first thing you knew, I had a carport full of "junk."

One of the biggest things I gave away was used toys. The poor kids had no toys and books. I remember the thrill of giving something to light up a child's face. Before you knew it (about 1962, I think), Mrs. Ruth Jacobs, a black lady and a Methodist I loved, asked me if I wanted to use her church to give out the things I gathered. I was so thrilled, but in those days the blacks and whites did not love each other, and I had a few whites come to the give-aways, but the black people were not too full of pride to come, and they all needed everything, and things were tight all around.

I soon outgrew the Methodist Church and moved to Fordyce to the fairgrounds. I was out in the rain at one give-away. Everything was getting wet, including me, and Clayton Crockran, who was next door in the National Guard Building with all the soldiers, came out and invited me in the building out of the rain. All the men started helping me take my boxes and items inside. That was the beginning of the National Guard give-aways. They only got bigger and bigger. Every time the people had something they didn't want for miles around, they brought it to me. The National Guardsmen were so good to me, and I had many food give-aways there when stores would give me food. In the 1980s, I started feeding people on Thanksgiving. There were many people who had no meal on Thanksgiving. It started out several hundred and grew to 1,000 and many volunteers helped me cook. I started about 4:00 a.m. When we outgrew the Armory, the cafetorium at Fordyce told me I could have use of their building, cooks and tables and chairs.

We invited everyone who was homeless, alone, had no one to eat with, or who was elderly or hard up in any way. This went on there for seven years and the big Thanksgiving give-aways, or a box of groceries with about thirty-five items for the holiday, started. We would start gathering food from the Rice Depot, food bank in Warren called the Bradley County Helping Hand, and the Boy Scouts started helping by staging a canned food drive. I would go outside on my porch and there would be a sack of food. Tyson Chicken people would give us, 5,000 pounds of chicken every Thanksgiving for the dressing, and a fellow café owner would cook all the turkeys we got donated and come at 5:00 a.m. and start slicing them as they were taken off his huge grill. One year, I had only one turkey and made 800 pounds of turkey and dressing from one turkey. That was in the very early days of the Thanksgiving dinners. I always made use of whatever I was given, and if I was not given so much, I "made do."

I never had too much or money or food to spare, but nothing was wasted or used for any purpose except good. I started in the days when dishonesty was unheard of and would not think of cheating or spending a penny for fraud. I do not remember when my food bank opened and there were no rules. If you and your family were hungry, we fed you. I never kept a Social Security number or asked questions. There was enough embarrassment to come for free food without begging or lying about the reason. I have seen little children come with mothers and slip food out of the bag and eat raw potatoes, who I knew were so hungry. Any man out of work or down on his luck for any reason did not have to go into a long, sad tale. He just had to help me lift, and some stayed and worked for their food. I never demanded it but always appreciated it.

Today the clothes give-aways are held in the Odell gym and about 2,000 to 3,000 people come, and we have donated furniture, mattresses, dishes, pots and pans, household items, clothes and maybe 5,000 pairs of shoes for the entire family.

I am now 73 years old and my daughter, Joannie and her son, Daniel live with us and are both involved in all we do. I want to "go out" wearing out and not rusting out. I never think about all the work, I just do. What in this vain world could mean more than seeing the faces of someone hungry light up with food being given to them? Hunger hurts, and cold hurts and hurts. If you had no car, no lights, no stove or way to cook, no money and no money for the doctor, and if you could manage the doctor there is no way you could get prescriptions, no shoes, underwear, clothes, food, what would you do? I have been the hope of many people, and I say "the poor have done more for me than I have done for them" because of the joy I feel inside in helping.

The Charity Letters

Dear Wonderful Friends,

It is 5 a.m. Sunday morning Dec. 28th, 1986. Christmas will be passed after today, and tomorrow. We have one more 13-year-old girl to take some Christmas to tomorrow, and today we have to pick-up some things at the hospital for some families. The ambulance driver's assistant, a young girl, called me...well actually it was her mother who called and ask, "are you the lady who was at the home where my daughter picked up a seizure victim Christmas day who went unconscious eating the Christmas dinner you had carried the family?" I told her "yes I was at a family's home on Christmas day... where the mother almost died chocking and I did call the ambulance." She said, "I knew when my daughter came home telling about the white lady who was there and the pitiful circumstances that it had to be the lady I saw a story about in the paper." So another contact has been made in the wonderful chain of caring folks who will give me things they can no longer use. The thrill of this is the ambulance lady is about the size of someone who needs clothes and shoes so badly! It is weird when I am sitting in a doctor's office or walking around shopping at the grocery, and I see someone and think "her (or his) clothes will fit so in so...wonder what they do with their castoffs?" I think it is against the law to "undress" some one in public! Ha.

I hardly know where to start telling you about December! I know, you all want to know and I try to send you a letter before the first of the year always, and if I do it I must do it today! I am supposed to leave for Pittsburg Wed. to buy a load of antiques. I am trying to beat the snow and get back the 14th for many who have appointments after that at the doctors. I so much wish I did not have to go because winter is so hard for so many, and they almost panic when I leave town, and I was just gone for a week the 12th of Dec. to the 19th...which is usually the busiest time of the year for me! But my daughter who was expecting was involved in an auto accident by a "hit and run" driver (he ran a stop sign and didn't stop) and she went into labor. The baby's heart was unable to stand the labor the monitor showed, so they had to do emergency surgery and take the baby. We went in great haste to the hospital in Nashville, Tenn. and the baby was born twenty minutes before we got there. We were there a week doing all we could for the baby and mother and father. When we came home "Santa" started! I got down on my knees in thankfulness to the Lord for Fordyce Bank and Trust. I had contacted them about the middle of Nov. I told them for twenty-some odd years I had carried Christmas to families in my area, and it had gradually become necessary to take care of families their Fordyce area too since the papers had publicized my work. I could not take care of all the needy this year...no way! I told them I had read their slogan for many years, "the Bank that cares!" I decided to test it! To make a long story short, they cared and they saved my life and gave joy to many, many! I had 51 families on my personal list, and the bank ran constant ads on the radio asking for toys for children and things for needy families in the area. They told them there would be a huge box at the bank and anyone, with a heart, could come drop toys or what ever in! This was started the first of December. Success is a mild word for the avalanche that followed! The bank also advertised anyone who knew a needy child to call in the name and location of the home. This also brought an avalanche of "new people" for me to "work." Some of the most needy I have ever seen. Some of the most neglected children I have ever seen. Some of the most hungry I have seen. Some of the coldest, worst housing I have seen...22 living in four (if you count the back) rooms with floors fallen in on the ground...almost. I have to go back to one house (especially) where the children seemed to have never been bathed! I am determined to find out why not, I can hardly stand it. They were barefooted, no coats or sweaters...Little Harvey lived here, and he is 3. He is so dirty, so poor, so dull eyed...so excited about the big huge pink rabbit you sent. I wished you could have seen him hug it to him and turn round and round. We have a tape of it. We are doing a video tape for the president and the Gov. of Arkansas...we will not be sending it until the Jan. clothes give-a-way. We are going to have one in the area that is the worst in my new territory! I am also asking the 22 girls at the bank to help in this. For the first time I will have help so can get it all sorted and hopefully can have transportation to carry mothers with boxes home. They can walk in but their packages are too heavy and bulky to leave, and I can never take them because it is only me. This will be the largest give-a-way ever and we are hoping for T.V. and radio coverage. If we have this then there should be an abundance of clothes given me next time. If I could ever get stock and helpers, I would try to keep folks coming one day a week for free clothes. But like it is I take all month long to those who need things so badly but only can open (generally) one day about every 8 to 10 weeks. There just is not enough of me to go around and no one hates to admit it more than me! I want to be superwoman so badly...but at 54 my back and hip and leg tell me what to do, often! But so many things you all sent were received with such special joy. I got home from Tenn. about 1 AM on Friday night the 19th, or rather the 20th, and that morning at 5 was up and started on Christmas. Cooking, cleaning and unpacking were forgotten, in fact, all my clothes are still packed and so are my husbands! It was planned we would have a Santa Claus, and he would ride in my van pick-up truck in the cab with me and one helper, and then three helpers would ride in the back and a lead car would lead us to addresses in a new territory they had gotten from advertising, but the day I worked the territory I had been for years working just Santa one helper and I would go. The bank followed my directions in how I had done the project for so many years...I would take the child and put his or her name on a white trash bag and fill it according to all I had available! Then all the trash bags for each family would be placed in a huge box and when the truck got filled with boxes I would go to that area and "dump." This is what they had done when I got back from Tenn. They had taken all the toys turned in and sorted according to names in trash bags marked. I carried up all the toys you had mailed me, and they sorted them.

I took candy you mailed and got much more, and we made many, many stockings which were actually brown paper bags of goodies. But oh! how the children loved this. When we started delivering on Monday, word went out that Santa was in town, and before long others were calling in and there were no toys. That night I started opening some boxes that came in in the last few days and had not been opened. Ruby Stewart had mailed candy, toys, and children's clothes and Rita Adams had mailed me about 100 children's books (at least) from a library that was getting rid of them I suppose, and we went back and gave books to every needy child and also we put in the sacks we were making up and delivering each day. Leta Dunn and Deane Dent and her friends had mailed some toys and all these were taken up to the bank, and in the conference room where millions are discussed, trash bags were spread and hearts and tears were discussed! We sorted and divided and just when it looked like some child would go without, a man or woman would hear the ad on radio (never had I been public before in giving toys away at Christmas), and they would bring an arm full to be sorted and taken to a waiting child. But a sad thing…some of the most needy did not contact the bank or me, and so many, many were left out…or some were discovered on our "rounds"…some would come up to the truck and say "why didn't you come to my house, Santa?" We were very sad about this – we tried to find where some lived and go without being asked by the parent or parents. This is the way we found Harvey and his family. We turned around here on Christmas Eve. We thought the house on each side of the road was abandoned. Low and behold, children started running out. The most pitiful of all the children we had seen. I cannot describe the dirt, shivering, neglected little bodies and matted hair. We determined to go back the next day. We did and video taped this. This is when Harvey got your rabbit, and we went to Wal-mart and got shoes for the family on each side…eight children in one house and six in the other house. Money was almost gone but Pat Brown, Roy Hatfield and Ms. Powell had mailed in some money the last days before Christmas, and we used some of this. Some of this money was also used to take a mother to the hospital to get medicine for her when I got her out on Friday. She had no Medicaid or SSI or help of any kind to take care of her bill. I have to take her back for a blood test Tue. before I leave town. I don't know how she will make it while I am gone but I will just pray about it and trust. My son and my husband will also be going with me.

It seemed from the first, you have been instruments of His peace because each time I needed you, and you were there with toys, clothes, money, or whatever. One family a society took care of. They have a little girl who had a liver transplant, and they needed everything. They have three under three, and the father had been without work... they had sold all their furniture trying to buy medicine before the child became eligible for Medicaid. The father went to work and got to work three days and backed over a piece of equipment on the job and almost castrated himself. I had the club call and ask if they could have a family for Christmas...boy! did I ever say YES! They took this little family and really were good to them. So you see with the bank, you all, and this society and many strangers this was the best year for helping so many.

Before I went to Tenn. a doctor in Little Rock called and wanted to take care of some children who had never been anywhere and who had no parents and would not have Christmas. He wanted to give them a nice present and feed them dinner at the Showbiz Pizza and take them on a tour of the City and the Capitol, of lights and some homes. He wanted to take care of ten. My husband and I could figure no time for this except Sunday, and after church we gathered the children who were ready and waiting. I had gone around and notified them on Saturday to be ready. We drove the 78 miles to L.R. and met the doctor and his girlfriend at Little Rock State Capitol. The joy these children experienced eating Pizza cannot be described. I was so touched when I saw one little girl picking up the scraps and hiding them. When the doctor saw this also, he sent me after ten boxes and he went to the counter and told the girl to fill the boxes with pizza for the children to carry home. They all were so happy and marked their boxes. They wanted their brothers and sisters and mothers to have a taste. My husband and I had taken two cars and were crowded at this...but this doctor gave the girls 4 foot tall Snoopy dogs and the boys huge bulldozers so we were really crowded starting home about 11 that night. It was a wonderful evening, and I think the children will remember this always. Hartsel and I got them there a little early so we went to a mall and let them see the beautiful things and get their picture with Santa Claus and ride the escalator for the first time in a department store. Seems they all like this always when we take a new bunch to town. Of course, the rushing shoppers hate this, but if I could only tell them when their faces reflect their anger at waiting for ten children to get to the bottom and get out of the way that these children will go back to cold homes, ragged beds full of other children and yards littered and porches falling down and no blankets and little food and sometimes beatings and abuse in everyway…and let them have a little fun for one evening. But you know very few of these folks would believe the lives these children have in AMERICA; there is no poverty some think! Even a lady told me that the Optimist Club had 25 baskets of food and could find no needy! I have no idea where these Optimists looked, but Monday morning I am calling the President of the Club and asking! They must have looked in the Heights and on Charlotte Street! 'Tis a shame…I think they WILL FIND THE POOR and are afraid of what they will see!

I want to thank a group of ladies who mailed things through Denna Dent! Oh! how much all the things you sent mean! As well as everyone else who mailed things! I also want to thank the Phillips in Little Rock for all the wonderful, fine clothes you came and had to unload yourself. I was in Tenn. having my first grandbaby and my son had to rush to Little Rock to my brother who has been very ill and had 85 percent of his stomach out the day you came Ms. Phillips. My mother had a stroke the first of Dec., and besides my own personal family sickness, all the children with problems had to be carried to specialists. So some of you came, and I was not home. Some of you called, and I was not here. Some of you offered some things, and I have not got to pick up the things yet, but I will. One man came Christmas Day and brought me a wringer washer from Fort Smith for a mother who tried to commit suicide a few weeks ago.

Thank you,
JoAnn Cayce

Dear Friends,

In the *Arkansas Democrat Gazette*, you had a news release in the Saturday's paper. I, first, want to make it perfectly clear I can't spell, type, and I can only give you 20 minutes this morning so can't use the dictionary! I am on no payroll, and I work three businesses. My days are long, very long and what I do, I do because of my love for people! America! Arkansas! ... and because I believe we are supposed to help one another! (in saying all this, I am not complaining, bragging, or killing time). The things I write here, or hope to write if someone doesn't come in, is not from imagination, books, education, but "field work." If you sit behind a desk, there is little hope you will ever find out things that will do you much good in helping the very people you are making the rules for! It is sorta like me telling someone how to raise children when I have never wiped a butt or a nose or lost my temper with a sassy child! I would love to tell you something that would "light your fire"! I work with so many unconcerned high salary, educated care-nothings that my temper is short and patience is next to nothing with run-arounds who think up ways to waste my time by "getting rid of me"...sicing me on another agency or program (that also says they can't help me but so-in-so will.)

We do need field workers in the development and health areas as no other area in all this land! I wish I could make someone out there understand that 70 percent or more of the people they are working with DO NOT READ, OR WRITE, AND ARE ALCOHOLIC. They have health problems you would not believe that are mostly brought on by wine, women, song, environmental conditions, ignorance, depression, confusion, too many children, too much money spent on the wrong thing, and no regular hours for ANYTHING! They have no idea what to eat, when to eat it, they have no medical treatment, and they take anything anyone tells them to buy at the drugstore if they can get the credit for same!

We do not need any more written material! It cannot be read by folks who cannot read, and I find it on the floors, in the littered yards or the baby chewing it up – if it ain't got pictures or me to explain it, forget it! The welfare depts. hate me, and the health dept. is losing patience fast. If you don't send some down-to-earth caring person who can communicate with the people they work with, and if they use terms and words they can't understand, forget it! I find these two things typical in most every person I work with who works with these folks. If the person is black they tend to want to show off for the folks they are suppose to help. They want them to think they are "something" — made it out of the trap of race prejudice. If the person is white, they are prejudiced and have the attitude "you are costing me, the taxpayer, and I am going to do as little for you as possible because I don't think you are deserving – you are the cause of your own condition!" I know this is dangerous for me to say this when I am writing to someone trying to get help, but if you see yourself in this CHANGE! You are working with human beings REAL PEOPLE whom in most cases are a victim of the system. The system is not working, and I am wearing out fast!

There are maggots in the ice boxes, roaches and rats in bed with the children. These folks need to tell them in no uncertain terms that if they don't spend the checks for better food and living conditions instead of whiskey, dope, sex or boyfriends someone is coming for the checks and the children! I cannot get children checked on, and there is no field work being done, and the children are being raised worse than my dogs – far worse. They are growing up to go to jail, have 8 more welfare children to be mistreated and raised to have more of the same! The children should be kept and given as much consideration as the car in the front yard...if the cars are not paid payments on, someone comes for the car!

Mothers do not know about ears to start at the bottom. They are hit on the ears, they never wash them, and I have a mother this morning who is pouring oil in her child's ear she mixed herself (of God only knows what) and she says when the ear busts it will be better! They need to be told how to have some regular hours for meals, sleeping, how the loud music they are playing right beside the baby's crib is deafening it! They need to be told that the whiskey bottles lying around with booze in them and the children are drinking it because they are thirsty or hungry can kill them. WIC programs for babies up to 5 years are just an escape for most agencies. They send the peanut butter and powered milk to children they never see and they do not know the child is home with a mouth so filled with sores and a butt so raw that it is something I leave and cry about all the way to the drug store! For heaven's sake – show films –talk – look at children. Do not give out food until you look at the children for blows, growths, lazy eyes, malnutrition, under-weight, deafness, and on and on. It takes only a minute to see deep switch marks on a deaf child that cannot mind if he can't hear. Warn them about sour milk in hot weather, leaving babies in hot cars. Show films about how hot it gets in a car. Tell them about abuse from uncles, boyfriends, fathers and what to do! Show films and pictures (remember they cannot read, and those who can won't). Don't give anything to anybody until you get your point across. Ask them questions and "if they ain't got it, do it again!" Like me – I ask if they have shoes. A child will say yes because he is embarrassed that he does not. Say "LET ME SEE THEM!" If they say they are in the car, at school, the dog got them, find him some more. I do the same for coats, sweaters, glasses, milk, eggs, medicine – I have to see it. Someone out there getting paid surely has been told in some of their training that proof is the only answer to questions! Tell mothers that throw- away diapers are not to be glued on a child for a week at a time. These diapers need to be issued with the WIC program with instructions on how to use them and what to do for raw butts should be like the peanut butter and powered milk! One teenager went for birth control pills. She got pregnant some months later. Do you know they handed her the pills and told her to USE THEM EVERY DAY! She did…she inserted one everyday! Why! Anyone should know they go where the fixture goes to prevent pregnancy!

Explain high blood pressure, explain chest pain, and explain bad headaches. A man had had a terrible head ache for three days several weeks ago. His retarded daughter ran two miles to get me; her father was down in the floor, dying with a stroke, and everyone knew his head had been hurting for days but no one thought it was important. EVERYONE HAS HEADACHES. The man did not drink and did not (usually) have headaches! You must get teenagers before someone else does. I cannot reach girls and tell them about the pills and get them to the health center and see that they take the pills, but a field worker working in the schools can! Sex education that is on their level and checks for VD should be as regular as the head lice they check for in school. Is one end less important than the other? Especially when a life is likely that will suffer and beget suffering on and on!

Please, please set up screening for diabetes, kidney infections, breast lumps and pap smears! Check all children on WIC program! They are dropped on a pile of rags when they are born, they are ignored for 5 years, all they hear is fighting and cursing, they fall asleep when they can't stay awake any longer, they cry out of hungry, fear, hate, confusion, pain, sickness for 5 long years. They are then dropped into a classroom with advantaged children and expected to compete! When they can't they are passed over. For 8 long years they are subjected to even worse than they had at home so they laugh too loud, talk smart, "be bad" give the teachers fits. Then they get one of two things – get in jail or get in the family way, and the thing is repeated all over again!

Start a war against tobacco, snuff dipping, cigarettes! If the tobacco folks have the Marlboro man, big as life and twice as nice, on the billboards, why can't we take a cancer victim or emphysema victim fighting for breath and down to 88 lbs and plaster it on billboards. With the man's tears flowing, let him say "I could have had a long life, but here I am enjoying another smoke and hoping I live to finish it…"

Explain what pork does to blood pressure, and, for heaven's sake, tell them that the medication the doctor gave them five years ago is not to be continued for life. Provide places in every community for blood pressure to be taken; do something when it is high; don't just give them a paper they will use for toilet paper – show them a film and scare them to death if they don't take the test seriously! Tell them the cheese the government gives them is not to be eaten day after day with their heart and pressure problems. Explain salt and what all that fat meat is doing to them. Many fat women don't know what is making them fat. They know it is eating too much, but too much WHAT? They think bread is fattening and grease, and other

"I done changed!" I don't know if he changed in five minutes or five months because they have been moved for about nine months, but I believe that Red Jack had a good Christmas, and he might have slipped the day after but if you can have hope once a year that is sometimes the star that sees you through and gets you to "lay the ax down!" Oh for a grain of hope for some of these souls!

I went up to take a dog a box to a young girl who was living in a trailer and had a dog tied out in the weather and rain and it was so pitiful. I went by there over and over and just could not stand it. I took a box and some warm blankets up there and knocked on the door. When she came to the door I…well I will have to be honest…I lied. I said, "I am from the humane society…you can't leave a dog tied out in the weather like that and not feed him and not water him and treat him this way…." I said "I have brought him a box, and if you don't keep him warm and hang a light bulb in here for him to stay warm by and don't feed him twice a day even if he ain't hungry, we are going to come and get that dog and you are going to be without a guard dog to tell you who is trying to break in on you!" I went and took the box out of the truck and set it up and took out the sack of dog food that I carry for strays along the road and filled a bowl up. I petted the dog and he came to life. He was talking to me and jumping, and she saw all this – watched like she could not believe all this. I just kept working. I then told her, "We folks that care about animals are serious, and I am coming back to check on this dog every few days, and if you come home and he is gone, you will know that the law picked him up." I have been by there over and over, and that dog is living like a king! Some folks just need educating and some can do better if they be scared a little! I wish there was more time to talk to you.

I love all of you,
JoAnn Cayce

Dear Faithful Friends,

Leta Dunn and Debbie Mathis, her daughter, made Barbie doll clothes and haunted shops for bargains in dolls, and you would never have believed what they came up with – Strawberry Shortcake and the works. The clothes they made were unbelievable. I took out the bridal gown from several packages and looked and wept to think these children had never seen a bride. Most are not born of brides but are an afterthought or a product of the alley or the field! It is heartbreaking to think of little girls playing with white gowns who will never know the meaning of the tradition. You know being born in America should entitle every child to love and a chance at decency should it not? This is what I base my roamings on. The little children deserve to believe there is a Santa and a better day! Then Sister Rhodes....made Cabbage Patch dolls....can you imagine Cabbage Patch dolls and preemies for Cabbage Patch Kids? I even had the papers to prove they had parents! Children who had babies that had two parents! Will miracles never cease?

Of course before I start telling you about the delivering, I want to report on Eddie. He is the little boy last year who didn't need your clothes, your shoes, your sweaters, or coats! Eddie hated every thing especially me! I was his biggest threat! When he looked at me he hurt so bad! Eddie knew what he had missed in life when he was close to me. He knew if he had been born to some other woman he might have had a loving and kind mother who cared that his feet were bare inside rags for shoes. His behind might have been covered in underwear under his jeans that did not fit. His belly-button might not have showed because he could not get his too small pants up far enough or his shrunken shirt down far enough. A "real" mother would have cared that his hands were cold, and that his teeth hurt, and that he had no birth certificate. It made Eddie mad at me 'cause

I made him know that he had nothing! I didn't mean for Eddie to find these things out through me but he had too! If I were to teach Eddie anything I had to start with the basics, and this was home and mother! His mother had man-hopped so that she finally managed to leave Eddie in a place where she forgot to go for him. He had been left in so many places and so many states that it was not hard for her to do! Lots of folks move so often they leave their dogs and cats behind – why should Eddie expect to be treated any better than the dogs and cats that roam the alleys and side roads? Eddie "never needed nothin'" to put it in his words. He had a shell around him ten foot thick, but then my life has been filled with lots of Eddies! I am a good nut-cracker. But I know it takes many different ways to crack the Eddies – sometimes something works on one but doesn't on another. Nothing I gave Eddie fit last year. He never would take a break when break-time came. We would all sit down, and I'd have them sandwiches and pop, but Eddie stood in the corner and kicked at something. I always wonder what they are kicking (most all of them do it all the time) I guess they are kicking at life. Eddie never needed a Snicker. He had to prove to me that he could go forever without a Snicker, without a woman, without a warm, clean bed! He "didn't need nothin'" he'd say! He even stole my money out of my cash register at the antique shop. He had to have done it, but what did a few quarters, dimes, and nickels mean to me? I was dealing in humans not small change. This same Eddie has been in and out of my life for over a year. Somewhere along the line, Eddie started listening. He would walk to the moon without a space suit for me now! I can't even look at something I want done, that he doesn't fly like Superman to do it! His "naw" turned into a "yes 'mam." He is now wearing (today) a pair of your size 8 cowboy boots. He don't have a hat, and his jeans are worn just the right amount, and his western shirt belonged to some of you yesterday, but today it covers Eddie's undershirt that was brand new – you sent it with the tag still on it – that meant a lot to Eddie. I don't know if Eddie ever had anything with a tag on it before.

Can you imagine these kids sometimes get something from you that is brand new, and they LEAVE the tag on it like they forgot it? That way everyone can see it is new! You see Minnie Pearl makes money from wearing her hat with the tag, but these kids make ability to cope by wearing tags on the outside! Eddie has tooth paste and a brush (I know because he carries this too in his pocket), and since he lives in a house that is not his (with 19 other folks – who hate his guts) his food stamps are his ticket to a bed with 4 others. Would you leave your tooth brush with them! Especially when you had 80 dollars it took you five months to save that you wanted to find your mother with before Christmas and give her a nice present, and someone stole it out of your knot hole while you were raking yards! But I asked Eddie when I took him his box, "Eddie can you imagine that someone loves you enough out there that they would send you a box of things, just for you?" (so I lied a little). He said "Yes, I can believe that!" I knew then I had won the battle with Eddie!! Last year he could believe in nothing – not even me he could see – this year he can believe in miracles he can't see! Praise the Lord!

As time got closer and closer to have the things you sent given out, I talked more and more to these kids who come by three and four times a week to see if there is work here or if I have been able to get them some after-school work. They were so excited about the holidays. They felt some one cared about them. Eddie came to me and told me about his cousin who was "moving in" – he was moving in with his girlfriend, and she had a two year old, and his cousin and her had a two week old. I went up there with Eddie. Sure enough they had just arrived. Eddie saw and heard me explain the WIC program and how this was a program that fed hungry babies but you had to go pick up the formula. Some of you had sent me six cans of SMA. I told them they had to keep that baby warm and dry and that it was a little human life and they had a responsibility to it. They were very surprised to hear this. Shock was there, plain for me to see! Even Eddie could not believe that it would be considered. Your baby clothes have gone to so many little babies who would have no warm clothes if it were not for you.

I was told there was a family back up in the woods who needed everything, and that they had three little babies. I started up there four days before Christmas with clothes. When I got to the road that turned off the rutted, muddied road I was on, I was met with a large black dog. He chased me all the way to the only house there in the woods. The mother came out...three toddlers behind in no shoes – they there the skinniest children I have yet to see. Big eyes.

I told her I was someone she did not know, and my name was not important but that folks gave me things to give away and what did she need. She looked like she was about to run, but then you picture the scene. I was standing in the rain holding a huge box, and the dog was barking his head off, and here was some dumb white woman trying to grab her children and run! I waited a few minutes and said, "Are your children going to have Christmas?" Now this is surely something she could relate too! "No," she said they wouldn't THIS YEAR….I hear this all the time. There will be nothing "this year." They never want to face the fact that there never has been and never will be! I told her, "Our people have mailed toys, and if you want some tell me, and I will see that Santa comes on Christmas Eve." I thought she was going to grab me. She started praising the Lord (a new switch) and saying that her husband worked but that he only got two days a week and made $20 a day, and it took that to pay the light bill. She wandered out in the rain with me and took the box of clothes. The dog stopped barking but got between me and the children that stepped out into the mud. I told her how smart the dog was, and she beamed. I am sure she thought "surely this woman can see we are fine folks…..we have a dog to guard the house and watch the children." I was wondering all the time if the dog had had rabies shots (which I KNEW THE ANSWER). I wondered how one so thin could bark so loud! Four days later I went back to take the toys, and as I started to turn down the last road I thought about the dog. No sooner had I though about him till I saw him. He was cold dead lying beside the road. I went on down to the house. I didn't tell the mother about the dog. I could not stop the laughter and hope in her face. I was going to let her have her moment. Who could tell how long it had been since she had sparkled like that. She would find out about the dog, and tomorrow she could cry! Today she was going to have her laughter.

This year I went to Mikael's house of course. Mikael had your sweat shirt with hood from last year on. It was hanging in rags but he looked up when I touched him and smiled. His hearing is gone, and his legs hold scars where he was beaten before I told them he could not hear. I took his clothes to him first and then later went back with toys. Remember the little airplane with the little people inside? Well Mikael sits and puts them in and takes them out! While the beer cans bend and the pot smoke swirls overhead, Mikael can forget what he doesn't understand and just put them in and take them out and send them on a journey and bring them back and land his plane and take off again! He has cars and a book and some colors and lots of candy! I looked at the dirt over him and knew his body would never be washed and his teeth would never be filled and his ears would never hear and I wondered why he had been cheated of so much in this life. I saw his skinned knee and thought how I'd love to take him home and bathe him and put monkey blood on his wound! Every boy deserves the joy of monkey blood being poured on his knees. The hoky poky fairy will never visit Mikael, and I had to stop the line of thought because I felt tears welling up. I snapped my switch and gave myself forty wacks because I have an agreement with self – I change the things I can, and I don't cry (much) for the things I can't. I would drown in tears if I allowed myself. I had to learn to swim and take the heat. It is hard to put food in an ice box with bugs, but it can be done. It is hard to take the lovely curtains you sent for the windows and spreads for the beds and put the curtains over windows that need to be torn out or are just hanging. You know, I thought you kept folks from looking in with these curtains you sent, and you kept the sunlight out, but now they stop some of the wind and snow and some are even nailed down all the way round. I hope this doesn't stop you from sending them because believe you me, the decorator for these homes finds it very appropriate. Your bath sets are sometimes covering a hole in the wall or nailed over one in the floor. A commode seat cover is covering the baby in a box that you mailed a miracle in. Many homes are now sucking your candy Mark and dreaming in front of a wood fire. Everyone had wood for Christmas. The old folks remember the days walking in the collard patch when the tumble bugs rolled the dung down the rows and the mule felt good and pulled the plow, and life was simple. The children dream of the toy they got and then wake to see if it is real.

With love,
JoAnn Cayce

Hello Everyone!

Will you believe I have a letter here on my desk that I started last April, another one started in June and after that I just gave up. You have been so very good and kind to me – to remember the poor here when I forgot you! So much has happened in 1987 that it is hard for me to even conceive that it was the biggest year ever for attention from the media and from even television. At first I said "no" to the Arkansas Community Service Award Committee when they notified me in March that I had been selected as one of the 8 volunteers to be recognized in the State of Ark. for my work with the poor. There were so many I needed to see about and so much I wanted to do with the summer, and I thought this thing is for the birds. But the more they talked, the more I became convinced that this might be a way the poor could be heard. The other 7 who were selected with the exception of one did not actually work with the poor. They were working with cancer, fund raising, Chamber of Commerce and this was the big reason I accepted the award and went through all the statewide attention and meetings and finally the big night on Channel 4 at the Excelsior Hotel in Little Rock. We were mailed a film of the night and there are copies available for $20. If any of you want a copy, I'll be glad to mail you one. The awards were presented, and the short speeches of acceptance were given. I did not know there was to be speeches, so I had a three minute off the cuff "talk" and kept it light to keep from crying! The best thing that came out of it was $500 to help with my "cause." The money went so fast I hardly knew it came in. So much good came from that $500, and some of those who benefited are still enjoying what was done for them. One child got his abscessed tooth pulled; some folks got a stove fixed so they could cook; we got lots of fruit and food and shoes and a baby bed; a little red wagon for a crippled child who had no wheelchair and never got to go outside. Now he is pulled around outdoors. He is four and has recently had surgery again on his spine. I had a female stray dog spayed and found it a home on the condition that this was done. These are the things I remember still.

My mother passed away in July. She had had Alzheimer's, and strokes also left her with no ability to walk or think or reason. I had spent nearly 11 months holding her in my arms. My sister came and relieved me in the afternoons, and this is when I did my work with the poor. I only thought I was busy the year before. With mother, there was no time to even brush my teeth! There was little sleep and lots of praying. Finally the Lord said "it is enough," and she had a massive stroke. There were no tears, then or since. I had a wonderful mother. I learned charity from her. She never took from life but gave. Every day she cooked a huge pot of something and found a hungry "somebody" to eat it. Every day was an opportunity to do something for someone else.

After Mother died there was so much time. I had a hard time adjusting to having time to run! I hardly knew where to start to pick up some of the things I had had to lay down. I did not lay down the sick or clothes or filling out papers but I did weed things out more.

Love to all,
JoAnn

Dear Friend,

I wanted to thank you with all my heart for the check we just received and your trust and love for this cause. I don't know what I would help people with if it were not for people who trust and want to help in this.

Just wanted to write you a letter and let you know I was thinking about you, and also I was thankful for your help. I have got to get out and get busy. No time to sit, ha. I am going to make a house-call to a 5-year-old little girl and will be carrying them some food and clothes for she and her two brothers. Their daddy deserted them and their mother is having a very hard time. She has gotten work now but no child support and food stamps are hard to come by if you work. I am trying to change this across Arkansas. I think a woman working who cannot feed her family should be rewarded for trying. They could stop working and have as much if not more. This lady is determined to show her husband he can leave with another woman and her children, but she will not let her children go hungry or naked. I share that determination with her. A family cleaned out their deep-freeze and gave her the food so they had food last week. She will get her paycheck today so we have made it through two hard weeks. She called me and said the five-year-old asked (from the pottie) "do we have no toilet tissue because daddy left?" To me that is a serious question, and I am using it to fight for a speedy case so these children will not have to wonder why they have no lunch money, toilet tissue, eggs, milk, bread, meat or lights.

Poverty is something single mothers fight daily and often time while the man is living without want. I don't know if you know, but no man can have a tax refund now if he owes child support. It will be given to his family. That took several years to get passed.

I met with the Arkansas Congressmen on Monday to try to stop the home health nurses from being taken out of the home, therefore forcing lots of elderly to go to nursing homes. They were supposed to be cut off the 9th. I think they will now change it. I believe if they continue I can get a protest to go to Washington. The ones who whack good things often keep spending that is pure waste. It takes lots of screaming. I don't know if you know that Dole made a speech that was printed in the Washington Post that there were no truly poor people in America, they could all work if they really wanted too. (There is very little work in our part of Arkansas (country). I stood before the Senate and House in Washington and invited Mr. Dole to our house and told him I could not afford an airplane ticket for him but I would buy him a Greyhound bus ticket, and if I did not prove to him there were truly poor people in America who could not find work of any kind, there was a dead cat in the well somewhere (in other words he would not admit it). It brought the Dirksen Building down and made the Post, but Dole did not come. The poor have little voice. I believe Jesus walked here among his poor children, and I believe they were his favorite people. When I have my clothes give-away every few weeks and they pour into the Armory when the doors fly open, I always think of the Pearly Gates flying open and the Saints coming in. Our children and grandchildren are greatly affected by their feelings for the poor. I am thankful to sweet Jesus for giving them this rather than hunger for great riches.

> Thanks again.
> I love you,
> JoAnn Cayce

Dear Helpful Friends,

I found a young couple with a new baby. They had no money for formula until Tuesday, which was 5 days away. I suppose they were going to let it wait. They said they were giving it water. They also had no disposable diapers. I went right to Wal-Mart to get supplies and milk. A check has come in from my charity letter this morning, and I want you all to know when your money is mailed God is timing it so prefect I am almost standing at the Post Office.

I am having a Mother's Day sale at the Antique Shop the 9th and a give-away the next weekend. I hope we will have a big box of food for everyone. We are giving food to families every day.

Today we are fixing food for a mother whose no-good husband left her with four beautiful little children, and my daughter met them at the ball field. She is trying to keep the two little boys in baseball. They have one uniform and one pair of shoes and one belt. She swaps them between games. They are 2, 7, 9, and 10. She has a truck that is going to have to go back this week. He left her with the payments, and she cannot pay them. This is a sad situation but everyday we run into families who are in such terrible shape. Sometimes the daddy is there but without work. Thank you for anything you send me. We need ties for the Retarded and Emotionally Disturbed children's school. They are having a prom in two weeks, and we need ties and white shirts for the boys from 12 to 17. We need white dresses for 5-year-old Head Start little girls who would wear sizes 5 and 7. We need sixth grade white dresses and 12th grade dresses. We have tried to help the school get underwear and when little girls come without, we are right there when we are called even if it has to come out of our own drawers.

I wanted to tell those of you who were so touched by the little skinny, ragged boy at the Easter party who said "I am really thankful for this day," he wears an 8 or 10 slim clothes, and he is also the little boy who entered the Halloween costume contest at school this last Halloween and they told him he could not enter that he had no costume on. He begged and said please let him enter...they finally saw how his heart was breaking and told him he could go on stage. When it came his turn he turned upside down and went on stage walking on his hands with his long skinny legs out and dropped like a spider. He announced "I am a crab" It brought the house down and he won. I predict that child will change the world someday. I wish I had ice cream for him everyday. I went by his house; it is clean and his mother seems a fine woman but they are very poor. He is a son to be proud of. He has no trouble at school and works hard.

I thank you so much for everything. I hope you don't think my causes are hopeless, and you will just give up. I spoke for Blue Cross and Blue Shield last week in thanking them for the Ageless Hero Award for Arkansas, and I told them volunteering will surely keep you alive. There are so many desperate cases out here there is just no time to die. God is good to me. I have had a chest cold, asthma this past week and this week, and I still have breath enough to go and do. I am so thankful. Tomorrow is Zoo Day. My disabled daughter is responsible for two neglected children who cannot talk and are retarded and will not get to go unless she goes. The doctor told her yesterday her hips will have to be replaced from her cancer but she is determined to go and take these children and help me. I think that is pure and simple love of children and people. I know what she feels. I wish I could ease the pain in every dark place I found it...it comes in so many forms. Much love and thank you so much...we will not waste a dime and we help our causes too.

JoAnn Cayce
Joannie Cayce

And grandson Daniel (he lifts a load everyday for his Granny and though hunger just breaks his heart he continues to help us give out food).

March 3, 1989

Dear Friend,

Time is a precious commodity around here! Sorry it has been so long since I wrote you and thanked you for the things you have done for me (others). Your help is a big encouragement to me! I do appreciate you so much. Just knowing you are out there is a great comfort to me. Sometimes, in years past, I felt so alone. Those were the days when I was "rooting hog" and almost dying from the pain of others and could do nothing. Publicity and accepting help was the hardest thing for me to do. I went for years day after day quietly "Begging!"

Since Christmas so much has happened. I will try to tell you a few things.

A man who trims trees called me a few weeks back and told me as he was coming in from work he saw a man hitch hiking with a baby in his arms. He stopped and asked the man where he was going. He said he was trying to get to the Health Department in Fordyce before it closed. It was raining and the man was about 8 miles from Fordyce and it was nearly 4 pm. The "tree" man picked them up and took them to the health office. He waited for the father to go in with the baby. They will not let a parent have a voucher for WIC, which is food for children, unless the child is brought in. The man had no transportation and no food and was forced to get out on the road in the rain with the baby. There are no provisions made in cases like his. I see this often and spend much time trying to help out in cases such as this.

When the father came out carrying the baby he had the voucher and the tree man told him to get in he would take him on to the store. It was getting late and the tree man didn't know what the father and child would do if he did not wait. When the father came out of the grocery store he had two cases of milk, juice and food and trying to carry the baby too. The tree man said, "You will never make it 9 miles in the rain carrying the baby and all that stuff." The young father said, "You do what you have to do." This touched the tree man's heart and he said, "I will take you back to your home."

He saw where the family lived and called me that night. He said it was very pitiful and thought I should go over there and see what I could do. I went over that next morning, and indeed they needed everything. I took food, clothes, helped with programs, the mother got a job at the Pizza Hut and things looked good. A week later the house caught fire and burned up and the young mother lost her 17-year-old brother, who was staying with them, in the fire. So now we start all over. This is the way it often is; I get a family out of one mess and things look good and troubles just seem to jump on them, worse than before. The same was the case of the 16-year-old from Bearden who lost her baby.

The school nurse called me from the school and said the children in school were poorly dressed and looked hungry even. She thought I should go down there. I went that same day. Indeed, things were pitiful. The dog tied on the front porch with no shelter was even starving. The mother had left the father because of his abuse to her and the children. She did not know her 16 year old was expecting at the time. The mother got work but later lost her job for taking off time when the baby was born. Things went from bad to worse. When I got down there the utilities were about to be shut off, the rent was overdue and eviction was pending, the food was gone and the water was to be shut off that day. It was cold and no winter clothes or shoes. The little four month old baby was smiling and reaching up to me even. It seemed to realize I was its only salvation. Boy if that doesn't make you work on a case nothing will!

I gathered what I could, called the local churches in the community, paid the water bill, electricity, and got the energy office to help with the heating bill. It was about to turn very cold. I went to Wal-Mart and got a big bag of dog food, took a box with rags in it for shelter, got food, clothes, shoes and started on jobs. Again things seemed to be looking up. I kept going down there, checking and doing for about two weeks. Work had been promised, and a family took one of the children to keep and had bought him shoes and clothes. He had had some trouble, so they were giving him the guidance he needed. I went to check on them on Tues. and went back on Wed. The baby was ill with a cold. They took it to the free clinic. They gave him his shots and told the teenage mother he just had a cold. He was worse the next day so she took him to the emergency room at the hospital in Camden. The doctor said he only had a cold. The mother told the Dr. that the baby had cried all night and all day and the doctor said it probably had a headache since the baby was rolling its head from side to side.

Just before day the next morning the baby went into convulsions and then a coma. He was carried to Children's Hospital in Little Rock where he died four days later. The entire family had stayed up there for four days without food waiting for the baby to die. They had left my phone number at home and did not know how to get me without it. I was so sick when I was called by the social worker when the baby died and they told the lady they needed to talk to JoAnn Cayce in Thornton. The mother asked me, "Mrs. Cayce what are we going to do with Bobby Joe?" Could I help she asked. I told her I would send for them and would take care of the arrangements. I went to the funeral home and ask if my credit was good for a four-month-old a burial and funeral and casket. They figured up everything and told me it would also be $60 to dig the grave and go after the little body. I told them to plan to do that and paid them $75 down. I went to get the mother and brought her back up to the funeral home to sign the papers, and then she and I went to Wal-Mart to pick out some clothes to bury Bobby Joe in. I was trying to handle it without emotion to keep the little mother from falling to pieces. I could tell she was on the verge of collapse. She had been four days without sleep or food. She said, "Mrs. Cayce what do you want me to spend?" I said get what you want and she said, "He never had nothing new." She said she had always wanted to get him something blue so she got a little blue suit, shirt, etc. We started to the check-out counter and she kept holding back. I finally said "Is there something else you want?" She said, "I wish I could get my pictures out of Bobby Joe." I asked, "Where are the pictures?" She said, "They are over there" and pointed toward the film section. We went over and got the pictures. We checked out and went to the car. How many times can a heart break? Mine has sure been tested. I watched her take them out in the car, and, as she looked and rubbed the baby's face, I just looked away at a starving horse across the way. I thought how much want there is in the world and so many complain because their hair won't do or there is not enough money for a new dress or the husband forgot Valentine's Day. Oh, what a screwed up world this is – where are the "real" needs? I thought I had some sitting right beside me. I hugged her and said "We are going to get Bobby Joe his first flowers to match his suit!" The florist hearing the story said, "Don't worry JoAnn, in the morning we will have a beautiful spray on top of the little casket", she did! Bobby Joe.... now had everything!

I was going to put the baby on my cemetery lot beside my grandmother. I thought this would have been very fitting. My dear grandmother had been abandoned by her husband in 1912 with eight little children in the dead of winter. My grandfather had run off with the lady who worked for him at his bakery. He had mortgaged all the furniture, house, business, took the only horse and buggy and skipped. My grandmother was put out in the street with the children and no where to go. She had 100 quarts of canned blackberries and about as many green beans and all over town there were frozen turnips in the ground. So they lived in an abandoned shack and had beans, frozen turnips cooked on open fire and blackberries. My Granny washed outside for folks who would let her children sit inside by the fire. They survived the winter except for her two little sons who died. When Granny died I felt very honored to have her placed on our lot because she had no place else. She was always so determined and stubborn that folks in the family who knew me and knew her said we were just alike! I always loved that. I thought many times when I came up against a "cold winter" with nothing but turnips, beans and blackberries.....it's been done before! This gave me courage many times to not "walk," but to dig (turnips)!

But when I returned home from the funeral home my husband had done some calling and he had a place for me to bury the baby. The City had a new cemetery with only one person buried in it and they would let me bury Bobby Joe there. The next morning I went for the family and took them to the funeral home and they all told Bobby Joe goodbye. The teenage mother was like all mothers, she was saying goodbye to a part of herself. We pulled her a chair up in front of the baby's coffin and she kissed Bobby Joe over and over. The

The 28-year-old who has not been out of the house in 12 years is better by far. She is getting an SSI check and has some new clothes that fit her huge frame. She has tapes, a TV, and record player and is up off the floor and sleeping on her new bed. I have them moved out of that shack, and they are in decent housing. The entire family seems to like each other, and it is a joy to go over and work with them. I am buying furniture as things are taken care of, and I have them a washer and dryer, and they are paying it out. The retarded brother is now also drawing a check, and he has stopped peeping windows, since I have him in workshop and he rides the van to Camden every day and comes in at night so tired all he can do is listen to his tapes and eat supper. I really talk to him. It may not be the way the counselors would, but at least he can understand me, and I don't think he will ever get in jail again.

I know you are all tired. I just want to tell you that I love each one of you and thanks for your continued support. Thanks for your trust. I know you wonder if your money goes in the right direction. I do too! I regret sometimes I can't write you the day I hear from you and tell you what I did with your check or what an encouragement your letter was but really the days are so short and I try to do my tape business at night and my antique business on weekends and run during the week so I can't always work you in, but thank you for not giving up on me. I am working on getting an old lady, who is 84, a better place to live. She refuses to leave her handmade old house. As it falls in she takes scraps she collects and picks up and props and rebuilds. I have some sober AA boys who are ready to start on her a cabin in front of this falling-in fire trap just as soon as we can gather the material. I would love to take some of you and show you her living conditions if you ever have the time. I know it would break your hearts, but in this way you may could help me reach someone with some nails, hammers, and roofing. Her kitchen is screen wire around some posts. I ask her how she cooked in there as cold as it was, and she said she only cooked on warmer days! Her mind is good and I hope to help her in days to come. Can't put this off too long because after all she is 84 and time is closing in on her, and the house is also falling in on her so we gotta move faster on this one.

JoAnn Cayce

July 6, 1989

Dear Friends,

I love each one of you and thank you with all my heart for all you have done for me since I wrote to you last. I have, so often, wanted to write you when I got clothes in the mail or by UPS or received a check at just the right time, but seemed there was no way I could stop at the moment and say thanks, but believe you me I said thanks to the good Lord, that is for sure!

Some of you had me pick up clothes in Little Rock at my daughter's house and some at churches or homes. Many left things on my porch while I was out running, and when I came home I often knew what was going to be in one of the bags or boxes before I opened it because of a great need I had prayed about that day or the day before. I often need shoes and come home and just the right size was in a bag or box on my porch. Today I had put off an unemployed sincere father who needed shoes so badly as long as I could put him off. I had waited for a nine and half size to come in, and it just did not come in. So I went to Wal-Mart and they had a great deal. They had reduced two pair of leather tennis in nine and half from $15 to $6. I grabbed them, and when I checked out and started home I thought "You dummy, what took you so long? The good Lord gave you $20 from an antique customer, and you still had $8 left." Sometimes I am so slow. I had toted the change around knowing a need would come up, and it did and I had to be hit over the head (heart) to see it. Anyway I brought the tennis shoes home to the man, and found his water line under his house had broken, and there was no money to fix it. This family of 7 was without water because "no parts, no money!" So you see I got shoes for feet and end up in debt for a plumbing job, but I should be glad I've got good credit.

I have been using some of your money to buy medicine for a heart patient who had surgery at the University Med Center. He had five by-passes and a value replacement, and since I was not around he was dismissed and no one to bring him the 80 miles home so he walked to the Freeway and hitched a ride and walked until he got to town, and then walked out to his country home. I don't know how he did this one week after such major surgery. His blood pressure is awful and he is trying to stay off alcohol (having no money does have its advantages), so he really needs his medication. So far I have not been able to get any program to fit his case – except you. Another man had a serious infection in his leg and it got in the blood and now he is on medication with no program to help him – of course he can't work, so this cost and then the most pitiful case: A grandmother went to take her grandchildren home to their mother, and a bunch of wild teenagers rode by fast as she was getting into her car about dusk to start home, and they stuck out a rifle and shot her in the leg, shattering the bone. This lady is in her forties and no money and no insurance and she, too, must have medication for blood clots that have developed and infection and needs a walker, etc…so of course I was called. When I got to her house the conditions were just terrible. No water, no beds, no screens, no front door, no tub to bathe the children who live there. This woman had taken in two people who had no home and no place to go. I am trying to help her get on SSI. Right now I have about six SSI cases pending. Three disability cases and about to file for three more SSI. I fill out papers every night and my husband teases me and tells me I am getting everyone on SSI. But I told him when the Government stops spending $340 for a commode seat and $850 for portable ashtrays, then I will think about stopping telling starving folks about SSI. I have just about every retarded child in the area on SSI. I can't understand why Social Services won't help folks get SSI but they don't.

These lives have been changed so much in the past months, and I want you to rejoice that you had a great part. Of course there are many cases I would love to help if there was means, and I am praying about this but I want you to know a little child who had no one caring for her now has a home with her great-grandmother and her sister. They are over 80-years-old, and with a 4-year-old to see to, their lives have changed so much. The child has clothes, toys, a bed (with mattress), shoes, and soon I am going to take a day and take the old ladies and the child to McDonald's in Camden, Ark. They have never been out of town or eaten out. I think two 80 some-odd ladies should have this opportunity before they die. Somehow death doesn't seem so bad if you have been to McDonalds or Andy's!

Speaking of Andy's, Mr. Street, who is an Andy's owner, gave me 25 free Andy burgers with Cokes! Man have I had a ball with these. I had a mother and daddy who called me to come see why the children could not stop crying and go to sleep. They thought they had ear ache. I knew something was fishy cause that many small children do not get the ear ache at the same time. I went over and at once I knew the problem. I said "When have these children eaten?" They said the stamps for the month had not come in, and they hoped they would come in the next day. Of course this is not the first time I have seen hungry children. I have gone and my husband has gone with me to take children food late at night, but I hope the day never comes when I can see it and not weep, or find a way to feed them. I went home and called my neighbor and together we got up a bag of things and then went for milk, juice and cookies at the store. The next day I started out with a list a mile long and people waiting, but first I went food gathering. That night that house was stuffed with food, the daddy was mowing my yard and the mother had two house-cleaning jobs for the week. They were willing to work but the father had lost his job and the mother had lost a child and had a nervous breakdown and had lost her job. Your money bought that food. This check came from some lovely and unselfish folks in Texas who had written a note and said "We thought we would be rich by now but it just hasn't happened." It had happened, long ago, so wonderfully and quickly they didn't even recognize it. The Lord had visited them with material things, but most important He had planted the concern and charity in their hearts. They had given unto the least of these, and the Lord says if we do that we have done it unto Him, and so they fed the Lord!

Another case you all helped me with is the mother whom I met begging food carrying a baby and five little potatoes about three years ago. I now have her in a house, with all the utilities, and some furniture and this week we were notified her SSI (she is retarded) is coming through in a few days (none too soon because her water is off and so is the electricity.) This just happened this month, and I did not know it until I went to give her the good news about her SSI! Ever seen a 90 pound mother with a baby in each arm shout on a porch that only God is holding together?

Many have wondered what ever happened to the mother with 10 children who was beaten by her husband, and we rushed her off in the night to a battered woman's shelter. Well her life is batting an 89. She is living in a housing project in Arkadelphia, and, with all her children, they knocked down a wall to the apartment next door, and now they have room, food, clothes, furniture and peace. You helped me get her over to the shelter and helped buy groceries for them the first few days until we could manage to work the details out.

A few days ago a man came to my house early in the morning. He had got a mowing job and the first pull got his hand in the mowing machine. He had no money, no way to go and did not know what to do but came to me. We were able to get his hand fixed with your money and a tetanus shot.

You helped me to get a little boy who started having seizures to Children's Hospital and looks like they have something started I was not able to do. I had reported his parent's neglect for years and to no avail because the child is retarded, and I have had to mainly see to him since he was born because his mother is retarded and his father an abusive alcoholic. Now Social Services is sending someone to this home every day to tend to the child, and I have gotten medicine and clothes and have him on all the programs now through what Children's helped me to do. I did not have the time to stay up there for four days but had no choice while they did a work-up on this child. But all in all it was quite an education for "ol' hand Luke" (me). I thought I had just about seen everything all these years, but when I took this deprived child (eight-years-old) into Children's Hospital, and he saw that mobile going up and down and all the toys and the friendly nurses and wheelchairs, light switches ON THE WALL (his lights were bulbs hanging from the ceiling), and he saw cars, trucks, and a helicopter right outside his window and even got to see it take off a couple of times, he went wild and just about climbed the walls. In fact two hours after we got to Children's Hospital the people in the same room ask them to have us move. How could I blame them? My charge was standing on the bed with the other child jumping up and down. He had never seen sheets, mattresses, roll up beds that also let down and water coming out of a faucet that was not just a hydrant. A million things you all take for granted were a great mystery to this child. I thought about the Tarzan shows I saw as a child and the plane crashed over the jungle and the baby was raised by apes and later was discovered by white hunters who took him back to civilization. This child's tray of food would arrive and he wanted to take everything off the tray and put it in the bed or in my pocket and then wear the tray on his head. He could not get over having a pillow. He carried it over the room and also the TV that was controlled from the bed. He was uncontrollable with this gadget. He ate three or four apples, bananas, drank chocolate milk and had meat all day. He gained four pounds in four days. He cried when we left. I had a time leaving him at his house when we came home. I sure did want to grab him and just leave! I often think how wonderful it would be if I could move children to where they "ought to be," then I feel so stupid! For some reason they were where they were, and who am I to question.

I have taken up enough of your time. I know you want to know the needs now so quickly I will just tell you a few: I have two little boys who are abused by the stepfather, and they are now at their grandfather's who is taking care of them well. They need another bike. There is one piece of one they ride on but they sure need another to go to town and to mow the few yards they have been able to get in town. They walk (about three miles) now. They are 12 and 14. I am having one of these children's teeth straightened in Camden. We worked on this project for two years, and it finally got approval so for some months now he has been going. It is hard sometimes to get him down there but I am committed. These little boys also need tennis shoes and jeans to start to school. I am watching the clothes that come in and soon will be giving out school clothes. If it were not for children's clothes coming in there would be practically no clothes in many households around here. I need $225 to help pay off a lady's teeth. I got a program to get her teeth pulled and then found out that there was nothing that would buy new dentures for her. I went out on the limb and told the dentist to go on and have them made. They will be put in her mouth in about two weeks and I don't have to have all the money right then but will need it quick as possible.

I need money for food, always. School is out and children get fed breakfast at school and then lunch, but now the ones who have no one to care and the ones whose families are so poor are not getting this food. Gardens have drowned out in some cases. Some families have beans and rice but children would love milk. I always need medicine money and gas money and money for glasses. A husband and wife now need glasses. Medicare will not buy glasses. The man is 66 and the lady draws nothing, she is 60. The eye doctor indicated he would help me but usually this means there will be no profit for him and that is his help. I did not pin him down because I had no money to go my part at the time. A man needs a battery for a 1964 pick-up truck (FORD).And I need shoes for a man who wears size 16. He is wearing 12's now.

I love you all. You encourage me greatly. I did want to tell you Greg, who is retarded, is doing fine at sheltered workshop. He is the young retarded boy I got out of jail several years ago. Irene, who also goes to sheltered workshop in Camden, has to be taken from her home this week. The police will come and move her tomorrow. Her mother beat her again with an extension cord and this time just about scared her for life. I told them enough was enough so they agreed, and she will be moving into her own apartment at Magnolia. She will be living in a complex of retarded citizens who are trying to live alone under strict management. I need not tell you how excited she was! She was slipped out and shown her apartment. Her mother would kill her if she knew, so everything is hush, hush. This girl is now 24 and has been a charge of mine all her life. It is with sadness that she will be so far from home, but Deena I did give her the clothes you gave me and they fit and she was so happy. I also got many practically new things "Poor Little Rich Girl" owned by Sally Streett, in Little Rock, gave me. Sally, many things you gave me right off your racks were for winter so I am saving them, but those that were for summer I have surely made many happy with them. You could have had a big sale but instead you gave these designer labels that were slightly used to little girls and young women who never could have had them otherwise. I had some who had just gotten jobs with nothing to wear. You are indeed going to be blessed with business, this I believe, so order up some deposit books from the bank. I think you will need them this winter! I often get a check or a box from one of you and just ask the Lord to give you so much material things to take the place of what you gave away that you will be amazed in wonderment! The Book says He is able to do above and beyond all we could think or ask.

For the benefit of those who think the world does not recognize little folks like me and cares less: the President of the United States just gave me (recently) a Presidential Citation signed by George Bush. I want you to know I have not had time to write him either, Ha. I was determined he would not get his "Thank you" before you all did; after all I have known you each in a closer way than him! You have walked with me in so many houses and stocked so many hungry stomachs and wiped so many tears and clothed so many naked little bodies. Please know I love each of you, and Yes, Virginia, there is a Santa Claus! Everyday I see him through your concern and your charity, may it never stop as long as you put it in my hands to do, and I'll do! No, I guess I would do anyway ...I did a long time and someway there was a way but you have made it so much easier! THANKS!!!!!!!!!!!!!!

Love,
JoAnn Cayce

November 9, 1989

Dear Friend,

This newsletter is long overdue, as most things I want to do are! I have written this in my heart many times, in fact, each day as I am driving in home I think of you all, and all you have allowed me to do with your donations or your clothes or your other things like an ice box, a piece of carpet, warm blankets, pots and pans, or toys and things for children. I always wish for you and wish you could have seen what your thoughtfulness and charity has done for someone, or a family. Most days are very emotion-packed. Some days are filled with questions that I can't answer and problems I can't solve, and often I feel like an ant trying to climb a mountain or swim the Atlantic Ocean, but as my old granny used to say "problems are solved just one step at a time in the right direction."

Since I wrote you last there have been many, many things that have been discouraging. But I try to look at the things that have been accomplished when I become discouraged. I continue to run the antique shop on weekends. I have a big sale coming up this weekend. I just got back from Pittsburg, Pa. with a truck and trailer filled with pretty things. I will get this sale over and hit it Monday at the bank, and then start the rounds. I have been home about 10 days and since then there has not been a day I have not had an emergency or a serious problem with a family. Heartbreak is something I never get used to seeing. With the cutbacks there are so few places to turn. In fact, Social Services have been turning to me to help them!!! I try, but as I told them a few days ago, I am able to paddle my own boat only by steadily continuing to keep dipping out the water.

About 11 months ago a mother came to me and wanted me to help her with an abortion. She was pitifully thin and had four babies already who were neglected and being raised in terrible circumstances.

I had managed to get the oldest taken from her because the boyfriend was not good to that child. The great-grandmother and her aged sister here in our town have this little girl and she is clean, cared for and loved though very, very poor and in need of clothes, etc. She is now four years old and we have managed to get her a ride to the four year old program (children can go if they have their own transportation which in rural areas is almost saying we are defeated before we are started). So the mother had three at home and she was 2 months again, no husband no decent housing, etc. I thought about this. I just do not believe in destroying life but I knew there was no future for the child whatsoever. I told the mother to go to the doctor and let him see what he thought and call me. The Doctor said she was five months, not two. That ended that as far as I was concerned but told her I would help her find a good home for the baby once it came. I insisted she stay off drugs, alcohol and sex with everything that came along.... I knew I was talking to the trees! When the baby came, a home was found and the child was left there for six months. On Friday the mother went to the lady who had the baby and told her the welfare sent her for the child. This was not true. She just wanted to file for the check the baby would receive if she had the child. She got the baby on Friday and on Sunday while under the influence of (you name it) drugs.... she beat the baby to death. I was called.

The baby's body was sent for an autopsy, the mother was taken to jail and finally foster homes were found for the other three children who were home when the baby was killed. The mother who had had the child until three days before it was killed was suffering greatly. She said there was nothing she could do when the real mother came for it. Of course she should have adopted it right away when the mother gave it to her but ignorance and lack of funds play a big part in trouble out here. I knew the baby's body would be coming back after the autopsy and unless I wanted to just let it be donated to science I had to be responsible for another baby's funeral. I had gotten the last baby's funeral and little stone paid for so I called Social Services to see if they would help me with funds. They said there was none, as I knew they would. There is always some rule or regulation that my situation doesn't match. Sometimes I really have run-ins with Social Services; also collectors that come to my door and stick out an envelope. I guess you can tell I am rather bitter about causes without effect! A food bank told me last week they could not help a family because they had been twice already! I told them any rule they had that cut out one hungry person was one rule too many! A good cause ruined by rules and regulations.

I am way off my subject: I went to the jail to get permission to plan a funeral, buy a casket and hire a minister and bury the baby. I had to protect myself and have the mother sign all rights to do this over to me. I thought, as I went to the jail: I just want them to lock her up and throw away the key! But when I went down to that old basement jail and ask to see the mother, and as they opened the door and the light from the hall was all the light that filtered in, and as I called to her she came to the bars with no shoes, no decent clothes and coming off drugs, and/or alcohol, no cigarettes, all alone and scared, realizing what she had done and not knowing what was going to happen to her, I remembered how it was when she was a tiny child, neglected, never knowing where she would be sleeping and with whom. Her mother was also a prostitute with a house full of dirty, hungry, unkept children. I had gone to that house many times and found children crying alone and hungry. I had to take hold of her skinny little arms and comfort her. She was a human, and God gave her life and even if she had done little with it I was not there to judge. I could not change events; I had to deal with the problems I could do something about. I told her I was going to bury little Jamie if she wanted me to. She started crying. She signed my paper, and I asked her about a minister. She wanted to go to the funeral and say goodbye to her baby. I told her we would try to work it out, but I knew that would be impossible. It was.

Several of you mailed me a check that week. I racked up $90 having enough to pay for everything. I also needed $250 to keep a mother and 8 children from being put out in the street. They were two months behind in the house rent. I managed these things this week when I got $30 from one of you and $75 from another and found a check for $50 that had been lost. I was also able to take care of another family who was in desperate need. The following is their story:

This mother had just come out of the battered women's shelter in Arkadelphia. Her husband had made the third serious attempt on her life by cutting her stomach almost out. She had been in the hospital and in the shelter for over three months. They had told her she would have to find a place to go and she had a sister near me. She came in after the shelter had put some gas in her old wreck of a car. She thought she could hide here, and her husband would not find her. She got here and her sister was gone to Calif. on a run. She and her husband drive an 18 wheel truck and the earthquake had hit out there and they could not get unloaded. So this battered mother was here with 6 little children and no food. She got in the house, and they ate all the food that was in the house. Five days later the two little blonde headed, blue eyed boys were telling folks on the sidewalk out in front of the house they were hungry. Someone called me. I went that morning. The two little boys met me on the sidewalk. They asked me, "Did you get us something to eat, we are hungry." I said, "I am going to feed you, but I have to see your mommy." They went running in and told the mother I was going to feed them. The mother was scared to death. It is hard to make someone understand you have come to help, not destroy. Can you imagine how hard it is for me to walk up to strangers and explain myself in three seconds? That is about all the time I have before the door is slammed or the screaming starts. When I got through to her that I was not about to take the children and I was not sent by her husband, and I was a doing person who would get food quickly, she fell against the door facing of the run-down house and started crying. The boys continued to pull at me and cry for food. I told her to let me go for food to feed them quickly and then we would talk. I went to my friends at the bakery and they gathered something up pretty quickly and I went for milk and they had orange juice in the box from the bakery so I took off back to the house. We sat the boys down, and they were wolfing it down as we talked. I had given them each a package with one dozen donuts in it and a bunch of bananas with 12 in it. We talked just a second, it seemed, and I turned to check on the three-and the four-year-old. The three-year-old had tears rolling down his checks and was stuffing the last of his bag of donuts in his mouth. I screamed to her "He has eaten all that bag of donuts!" I counted, and the three-year-old had eaten all his 12 donuts and 4 bananas and the four-year-old had eaten all his donuts and either 4 or 5 bananas. The mother said, "Mrs. Cayce will they swell up?" I said, "I will take them to the doctor if they get sick. I started the rounds of my friends because I had very little money and I told them I had to get groceries quickly for a family. I went to Social Services first, and they said it would take several weeks to get food stamps. They would have to check on her situation. I told them if her husband found her he would kill her and possibly the children. I went to the food bank, and they said the mother had been there twice already and they had a rule they could only come twice (I will go to the next board meeting, I hope).I was able to come up with $86. Then I went to the grocery store that helps and gives me things that are old, etc. I told the manager I wanted something good. I said I don't want any rotten apples or bad potatoes today; I need some good things for children who have had nothing in five days. The mother told me that they had eaten the Friday before. She had gone to the 7-Eleven and asked them to hold her drivers license for a gallon of milk and two dozen eggs. Of course the older children were going to school but they were not yet on the free lunch program. I thought it was pretty smart of the mother to think of getting food that way. The grocery manager gave me $20 and said, "Buy anything you want." I was tickled. I shopped and shopped. I went back to the house loaded down. I later took clothes, etc. I made application for the little ones to get on the WIC program at the health center, and things will all be worked out for this family, it just will take awhile. I had her old car filled with gas. It took $21 to fill it so, I would say there were not even any fumes in the tank.

Halloween was this week, so I had a wonderful time trick or treating. Our son-in-law came and he treated here at the house, but my daughter and I took their son who is two and 3/4 and took treats to children who cannot get out and trick or treat. Some are retarded children who have no one to take them and some are so needy and neglected they have no one to care about things like this. They were delighted to see us at the door. This afternoon I plan to go to the jail and carry warm sweaters (your gift to them, not mine, I am just the delivery boy) and some clothes. I will take all the candy we had left and gum and other things to the prisoners. I hope you all understand this. I am criticized for things like this sometimes, but again, I am not a judge in their cases. If I relieve human suffering I have to go where humans are suffering. Sometimes I find them suffering in strange places. I am not comparing myself to Jesus, I would never do that, and I don't peddle religion, I am not in that business either; but I take comfort that the Master, in His examples which He set forth went many places He was criticized for. I think more than once He was accused of keeping company with publicans and sinners. I keep company with myself, so I am keeping company with a sinner, if I don't get out of and away from my own self.

Over and over this past week I was called out before day by an emergency. A child had a terrible toothache one morning and I got a dentist to see him and the abscess was worse than he thought and the next morning the child was in terrible condition, swelled to explode. We got that taken care of, and two days later the welfare was trying to take his sister's twin girls. The sister is 15. She was 14 when the babies were born. They are neglected and unkept. I have tried to talk to the girl and to her mother. I ask the girl if she wanted them or if she had rather someone take them who would feed them and care for them. She said she loved them, but I told her that was not enough, she had to care for them, they could not survive on love. We got that temporarily taken care of. Then a poor man had a heart attack, and on and on.... there is no let-up.

Many of you may want to know about Terry. He is doing better. His leg is still very painful and I weep for the injustice that was done him, and I debate if we should hire a lawyer or not. For those of you who do not know Terry, he is the one I got a dentist to start straightening his teeth. His life has changed since I am spending some time with him, and his mouth is going to look decent. He has some clothes, and he has someone to listen to him tell how mean his stepfather is to him and all his problems. He was in the woods with his stepfather and they were cutting wood for the winter and using a metal wedge and a ball peen hammer. A piece of the metal came off the wedge and went into Terry's leg. It severed an artery in the leg and the blood was gushing. The stepfather carried him to a doctor who called in a jack-leg surgeon who had blown into town some months before. He had the hospital take some X-rays and these showed plainly the metal missed the bone and was on the left side of the left leg. The man cut on the right side of the left leg and severed the artery on that side. It is beyond me how such a mistake could have been made. He was rushed by ambulance to Pine Bluff and the surgeon there had a heck of a time saving Terry because he had lost so much blood. He was up there about ten days. I took him to the dentist yesterday and when we started to leave town I ask him if he wanted anything to eat. He looked at me really scared and said, "Mrs. Cayce do you think you could buy me a milkshake?" I think it was his first and he is 14. I got the largest one they had and he was a sight for overflowing heart to watch him suck his straw and play with it. One thing about the poor, especially poor children, if they get something they have never had before and are enjoying it they will make it last as long as possible. I have seen starving children pinch off tiny bits of a slice of bread or cookie to make it last and last.

Christmas will soon be here and I am caught with a bare bank account. I have collected some toys and have these. I want to start washing and dressing at night some of the toys you have given me. I do hope that Wal-Mart will let me put a bin there as they did last year. In rural areas there is just no organizations that take care of this thing. I hope the bank will help by allowing me to put a bin there. They have allowed this for three years now. The list is longer this year and there are more and more white families needing help. So many need medicine and Medicaid cards are so hard to get for the sick. I have a crippled child going to Children's Hospital this week, and I hope they will see this child free. I have a father who has a severely crippled two-year-old, and Children's Hospital is threatening to sue him for a $2,000 hospital bill that he has not been able to pay. His baby had an accident in the Nursery of the Pine Bluff Hospital and was transferred to Children's Hospital and the father cannot pay the bill. It is hard to get help even for children this day and time. I have a mother who has a mass in her stomach and she needs someone to see about it. She has no money and no where to turn. I cannot get a Medicaid card for her. The doctor found the mass and said it had to be followed up, but she can't get anyone to see her without money. This is just one of many. If anyone knows who might help, let me know.

I love each one of you so much. You have done so much for others. I am ashamed that I was not able to do more with what you sent but it seems as fast as it came in, it went out. I have been able to get more clothes, however, and I am so thankful for that. Of course I need about 500 blankets for winter to give out. It is strange there are Government programs that give out fans in the summer but they do not give out blankets in the winter, or if they do the news has not reached me.

God bless each one of you, and may you have a wonderful, safe, happy, fun and food-filled Christmas. If any of you have things you wish picked up in Little Rock, call Joannie at 565-4214. She will make arrangements with you for you to bring it to her house. We will pick it up there. My daughter, Kandy, lives in North Little Rock, and she will be happy to bring it to us or keep it until we can pick it up. Her number is 835-3013. She works in the daytime. Joannie is disabled and is home all day but she is on the bed all afternoon and her phone is off the hook. (The doctors have her on bed rest all afternoon.) Call her in the morning, the best time to call her is between 10:30 and 12:30. Our daughter, Gay lives at Arkadelphia, AR. and her number is 246-7376. If you have things you wish to carry to her house, give her a call. All our children love helping in my projects.

JoAnn Cayce

ain't hunted in a very long time 'cause I can't walk to hunt and I don't have no money for shells anyway." The Judge then said "I ask you if you liked to hunt and you said you did." Herman said "I does." You know some folks are educated idiots! They are so far removed from the common man they might as well be on another planet. There are human beings with feelings and needs left in this world who may have a body that smells, a plank to sit on instead of a chair and a bed made from rags they gathered at the dump but they can tell us more about patience, making do, doing without, and strength than many who stand over them as "judges." I touch misery every day and I try to learn from it.

Two children whose mother had left them lost all they had left, their home and their father in a fire a few days before Christmas. These were poor folks. Thank you for the new clothes, food, shoes and Christmas they had. As I stood in the ashes of this loss I was comforted, there would a Christmas, I was already planning it! THANKS TO YOU!

We did get two cases approved: Phillip ----- who called me four months ago, late one night and said he was going to kill himself. He now has a new lease on life, is sober, on disability and can't believe his "luck." He sent me one of the best Christmas cards I received. On cheap paper he said "thank you Mrs. Cayce for all this family (he and his 82 year old mother live alone) has, because you cared, we will eat this year and be warm." And James ----- got his SSI and Medicaid. This homeless retarded man came to my clothes give-away for clothes and shoes. He was so thin I ask questions and found he was sleeping in an alley. He now has an apartment in low rent housing and furniture you gave me makes his "home." A table and chairs was all he lacked, and a few days before Christmas the Sherwood Family Clinic people came and brought one. I told him to come on Monday after the 15th, that they may bring one and they did. He was here and the table and chairs makes his home complete. He can't speak much but his grin is a mile wide. If happiness could be bottled he would be my best supply. I'd put a spout on him and just keep filling bottles and passing it out!

I didn't make it (yet) with Mary, Herman, or Freddy -----, but the negatives have a way of turning into positives in the strangest way. I'm waiting!

Each month there has been a clothes give-away in a different place and your things and what is left on my porch turn out to be the greatest blessings for people. The ladies from Kentucky have been here three times since you heard from me last. I can't believe they remain so faithful! They really are my special gift! The army has given them a building in Fort Knox and they collect everything anyone gives them and puts in this warehouse, then they come all this way to bring it. I like to think the gold is not all in a Fort Knox vault! A lot of wonderful women (mostly officer's wives) and a lot of used clothes are stored there too, and God gave them to me! Who needs gold with charity like this?

Of course, since I wrote you there have been some child abuse cases, a nine-year-old and an 11-year-old raped both by a step-father and a father. In these cases the mothers moved out and this left a family without a place who had to have a new start. There are no provisions for "new starts" in the "system." Still takes about 45 days for food stamps and up to two years for HUD rental assistance. AFDC is so hard to get started for children and in most of these cases the family leaves without clothes, shoes, school supplies, and transportation; items like skillets, dolls, toothbrushes and coffee pots. So you see your blankets, spreads, pillows, bath towels (no matter how worn) are God sent. More and more folks come or are sent to me for help. This past week the Community Action for our county called and a family burned out without insurance. The father also dropped dead. The children had nothing to wear to the funeral. So even if it were Christmas, and I was knee deep in toys, everything has to progress at the same time. Again this Christmas I sat in the emergency room. This year it was a case of blood poison. The doctor came in and went right to work, but not before he said "Merry Christmas JoAnn, I think we have spent the last three together." I said to myself "That is all the years you have been with me." I have been there, or a member of my family, or my husband most every Christmas holiday. Sometimes my husband and I have spent the holidays chasing ambulances. Then the day after Christmas a 14-year-old took a bottle of 100 aspirins. If it had been Tylenols would have killed him. I had just had this child evaluated a few weeks before and had just gotten the letter from Social Security that there were no mental or behavior problems. Sort of like the child a month ago who had no eye problems, but I insisted on getting the child to Children's and they will do surgery the 9th. It ain't that I am so smart it is the evidence is so overwhelming! Too, this gut feeling that grabs me and won't let go! If you ever get it, don't let anyone tell you it isn't there. If you do, you will be sorry! I saw Donny after his stomach had been pumped and ask him why? He said he was tired doing without everything. This mother has a 15-year-old daughter who just had a baby and now a son who tried to kill himself.

A few weeks ago the retarded school in the area called and said they had a young kid who had been brought in and there was no check coming in yet. He had no shoes or clothes. I told them I was taking two more boys to Wal-Mart who had been beaten up by their step-dad who had no shoes so we all met there. Clarence just could not understand it all! He got new jeans, shirts, socks, underwear and an "odd" lady measured and tried on tennis shoes. She joked and laughed and talked fast. He didn't know what was going on. I ask Clarence what size shoe he wore. He said 8. Sure enough, I looked at his old one and it was an 8! But looked at his foot and knew it was a 10 1/2 or 11. Turned out the fourteen-year-old had an 11 foot in a size eight shoe. I knew he hurt so bad it didn't matter what size shoe was on his foot. It took his mind off his real pain. I have seen this before, but I never can accept it without pain. We tried on jeans in the dressing room, and if you have never tried on clothes at Wal-Mart, the dressing rooms are really tall round barrels that lock on the outside. Why? I don't know. But Clarence got locked in and while someone hunted for the key Clarence and I really got acquainted through the locked door. He had never had new things before. We checked out with three piles, one for each kid. The two "local boys" were used to me, but this "new kid" could not figure it all out. He kept asking "where do you work?" I finally told him "I never had a job in my life." Then he asked again who I was. He was really desperate so I said "I work for nice kids like you." He said "No, lady, why are you doing this?" (Now that is the hardest question of all and the one I am most often ask.) I just hugged him and said "'cause I get to know the nicest people just like you..." It was the hug that did it! Then he was like a leech!

When we finally had to part, two kids and me one way and Clarence and the school van and counselor the other way. Clarence kept walking backward and looking at us and waving. Finally he yelled "Lady, thank you." Clarence's family didn't send for him or come to the school to get him for Christmas, but there were nine in all who had no family who wanted them. This is less than last year. I think we had 19 last year at the Christmas party who had no place to go. Thank you for sending the donations that footed the bill at Wal-Mart, not only that day (which was nearly $200) but for all the Wal-Mart bills during 1990. I wish Mr. Walton knew how much and what I did with the things I got from him. He might give me a discount. I went in during December and bought all the basketballs they had. When you push two baskets filled with basketballs through the check-out and no one thinks anything about you doing it, you realize folks expect to see that "crazy lady" being crazy again! When I go into Chicken Country or McDonald's and get thirty-five chicken legs or 50 McDonald's 59¢ hamburgers to go and ask them to put them all in separate bags its hard to keep people thinking you are sane. You get a reputation for being a nut! It's wonderful to be able to be yourself.

I ran in Wal-Mart the other day in a big hurry to buy about 6 cartons of diapers in different sizes. One of my "friends" asked me grinning "Expecting something, Mrs. Cayce?" I said "No my dear, it is already here so move it, will you?"

The first of December I took a lady having many seizures each day to the University out-patient clinic and a child to Children's Hospital day clinic. I was overloaded and knew it but had no choice. The lady had 7 violent seizures where she literally beat me with her fist without realizing what she was doing. One of these was at Children's in the lobby with everyone looking on. As I tried to calm her I thought "things can't get any worse than this." Every time I think this, two minutes later I am sorry. This was the case. The fire alarm sounded and fire drill started with everyone yelling "is this real?" No one ask that question louder than me. Can you imagine trying to hold onto a child who has never been in a cafetorium and lead a retarded woman down a serving line pushing two trays at the same time? (My doctor wonders why I have migraines.)

I want to tell you about Thanksgiving! We fed 356. It was a wonderful Thanksgiving! I got to feed more than ever fed before. I hope I get to do this next year.

January 2, 1992

Dear Friends,

All through the house not a creature is stirring, not even a mouse (well maybe . . .) 326 little children have some similarity of Christmas presents. I, of course, sorted all year and saved toys, but there is no way I can find enough good toys for this many children out of what folks discard. I have you to thank for making it possible to care for so many.

I take the toys that are not "too good" and give them away at my clothes give-aways all year and keep the "better part" for this time of the year. I get panicky about the middle of November knowing so many depend on me for Christmas. Some "third generations" are receiving bags of Christmas toys and clothes through my efforts and your charity now. This shows you how poverty is passed down and how the ways of the parents are taught the children. Of course, about 75 percent are new families each year have fallen into situations they cannot control or have no ability to climb out on their own. Many have families who are no better off than they are, to help them. You and I are the only "family" they can call on for help!

Our family had our tree and dinner on the 26th of December. We delivered until 7:00 p.m. on Christmas Day night. We were giving out bags to emergency cases. One mother got out of the hospital, one father had a tree fall on him and got out of hospital, one mother thought she would get paid at her new job before the holiday and didn't. Some pretty far away called because they had heard about us and until then did not know what to do. The night of the 24th of December we kept our porch light on, and one family came for a bike for a little boy whose father was in prison. A doctor in Little Rock made it possible for us to get him a new bike. He only wanted a bike. The mother is alcoholic, and his 14-year-old-sister has just had a new baby. I felt he had to have this new bike. This was the only new bike we purchased this year. We did have three used bikes to give out. Another family got their Christmas from our porch swing late, another from the front seat of my car, another from the front porch of my husband's office next door and still another came for theirs on the side porch of the house. But most families came for their children's bags at the National Guard Armory the 20th of December. We had bags of apples, oranges, candy that went with each trash bag of toys and sweaters and coats. We also had socks, shirts, warm-up suits and school supplies purchased with your donations. Some children had no shoes, and if we knew about this we tired to help this situation.

Boxes of food were given out with food folks put on my porch or had me pick up or brought to the antique shop. We had some left from feeding the 620 for Thanksgiving. This dinner was cooked at the National Guard Armory and was a record turnout. 146 dinners were delivered to the old, crippled, disabled, shut-ins, and lonely. Thirty-nine volunteers helped carry out this seemingly impossible task.

There were many touching things this Christmas: I had a mammogram that showed a possible problem, and a doctor at the Cancer Institute in Little Rock saw me several times, but on the 19th said he wanted me back the next morning at 8:00 a.m. for a biopsy. I said, "I just cannot drive the 75 miles up here in the morning." He had gone out of his way to see me, and I could see him turning red from his shirt collar to the top of his head. I looked him in the eye (not knowing I was looking into his heart) and said, "I have sorted toys and prepared bags for over 300 very poor children and their people will be picking them up all day tomorrow and if I am not there to give them out these children will have no Christmas." This busy doctor melted. He said "A few more days won't make a difference . . . see that these little children have Christmas." I watched his anger turn to compassion, and it touched me deeply.

One crippled man came for thirds for his children and told me he was going to have a wonderful Christmas with his wife and six children, and he was going to hitch-hike to see them. I, nosey as I am, said, "Where is your family?" He said that he was hurt on his job. He was crippled and had a concussion. He could not work so they had to live apart so they could get aid: food stamps and AFDC.

This poor ignorant man had signed a settlement for almost nothing and now cannot work. If he stays with his family they will get no aid he said. I think all this can be changed with someone working on his case, but it will surely be long and drawn out. Human Services, Workers Comp and Social Security will each be a case. The man is so injured he cannot remember one minute to the next. He has forgotten how to read or write. Of course, I doubt he ever was able to do more than just enough to get by. He was so happy over the bags of things but he could not carry everything. If he did not get a ride he would have to walk and he took only what he could carry. He was 60 miles from where his family lived.

It seemed as we needed things, they just "dropped from the sky." Some of you gave me late donations, and when I thought there was no way, you made a way. The 26th of December we gave out things to three families who heard about us, and these were things that were left on our porch that morning while we were having our own tree and did not hear the door bell. Many things were mailed and some were carried to one of my two daughter's homes in Little Rock. KSSN Radio in Little Rock, and the Whetstone Law Firm, and several doctors enabled me to do so many things that would have been impossible without them. Then there were several other law firms and one family who used to live here who remembered the poverty here. They touched me deeply with their donations. One law firm has offered free services to get me a tax deductible permit so your donations can be legally deducted on your taxes. This will be wonderful and will help me get more help. Sometimes I need a man to lift and help me so badly. My lifting days are about past.

This year we did something we had never done before. I had tons and tons (literally) stacked in my warehouse of good warm clothes that did not get given out in November or December because of my daughter's illness and surgery, my knee surgery and the Thanksgiving efforts. I took on the feat of getting this out before Christmas. We had a clothes give-away on Saturday before Christmas. It was the biggest turn out I had ever had. We gave away about 5 (at least) tons of clothing and lots of miscellaneous items such as dishes, mattresses, chairs, curtains, sheets, blankets, our cull toys, fruit, baby formula, candy, shoes, pots and pans. Some helped with this effort who had never seen one of these give-aways before. They came to me and told me they had never been so touched. These people said they had things they threw away they never knew anyone could use. Several poor brought me Christmas cards to this give-away and some made me things out of scraps, and one alcoholic brought me a decorated whiskey bottle disguised! He gave it to me with tears and a white lie saying someone gave it to him and he "fixed it up." This brought tears and laughter. One family walked; brought me a "used" Christmas card and each one had signed their name and tried to write words of "love." I never saw sweet messages so misspelled before.

I hope you will all know what you mailed was used, and I even have a balance in the charity account to help some have heat, medicine, doctors, transportation, and take care of emergencies in January and February. (I know the bad weather is bound to hit soon). We had a family with 6 little children burn out just before the holidays. You helped provide food and cover and a stove. I never have much money to operate with. I know this keeps me humble, but to come through Christmas with a balance is a miracle. I have a pair of glasses I want to buy for a young man.

I took two boys, one 14 and one 16, to Wal-Mart several nights before Christmas to buy their Christmas (with their own money). They are among the children who I have been appointed guardian for. I had saved some from each month's check for their Christmas. They picked out a bike, a pair of new school shoes and a coat. They could not believe they were getting these things (this is the first year with me, for them), and I told them they had $41 left and was there something else they wanted or did they want the money to buy their step-father and mother something. One looked down at the floor and wanted to know if there was a bottle of something in the store that smelled good he could buy to wear to school. I said sure and pointed where to go get it and we would wait. He came back and said, "She will not let me bring it to the check-out counter unless I pay for it there." I went to the cosmetic section and told the lady I wanted to get the cologne Terry picked out to pay for it with the bikes up front. She said, "Mrs. Cayce I didn't know he was one of your boys." For just a minute I thought I would give her a lesson in trust. Just because a teenager was ragged, black, had no coat and run over tennis shoes was no sign he could not be trusted with a bottle of cheap cologne to walk to the check-out counter. But then

I thought the embarrassment she suffered when I came to pick it up was enough.

I especially want to thank Jan for the money she mailed and the extra to buy size 17 shoes for the 7'3" abnormal boy. We got shoes and a nice coat and some food for him. He has been to my house twice – wanted to "work" thanking me. I told him over and over it was not from me. He did some lifting for me and helped me help others.

Again, thank you for all you have done to support me! I ask you to remember me and my people. Many have lost jobs and some are starting lives over without abusive husbands. Some are children in different homes, and some are disabled who will need a miracle to survive. Some are alcoholics who are determined to be free of the habit that has stolen their lives. A few are homeless and are in temporary homes. I have filed SSI for them. Coming up in January, some will stand before the Federal Law Judge at their hearing. I will represent them as their non-attorney. I want to be able to fill all the appointments on my calendar now and hopefully fill others as they are made. I need health to do this. Don't take for granted you are healthy, always. I should know this since I have a daughter who has fought for her life ten years now. Somehow I thought because I am needed I would remain healthy. Pray this is true! I will be more humble and thankful and appreciate more since I am threatened.

I love each of you. You are the strength under my wings but I know the Good Lord holds us both in the sky. You would not have it to give and I could not "fly" without the blessing from above. Happy New Year. Thanks again!

In love,
JoAnn Cayce

September 23, 1992

Dear Precious Friends:

Would you believe in the morning I am driving (alone) to Pittsburgh, PA to purchase stock for my Antique Shop? I wanted to write each of my friends who have been interested in my work and my people. I think it was last November, 1991, since I wrote a report. I know some of you have wondered if I were still "in the poor business." Yep! The poor are still with us as the Bible says! Some have died, and I must think "they aren't hungry or doing without electricity or medication any more," but in some ways I feel I have failed them.

This is not going to be a morbid letter – I want to tell you funny things too. I wanted to let you hear before I leave and tell you about plans I have for the rest of the year and what has happened in the past few months.

Maybe I should go from tonight back. I don't know if any of you remember Ida Mae. She is Ida Mae ----- now. The man, who had the stroke and was alone, and she got married. If you remember she was going to his house (at my request) bathing him, feeding him and cleaning for him. She called me one day and said she had him up walking. I could not believe it. Sure enough he was not only standing but he was talking (a little) walking and wanting to go outside. She thinks it is the massages she gave him and the turnip greens! They go to the post office holding hands (he is 67 and she is about 50). She says, "He can't remember having had the stroke, but then he can't remember anything else either." She is retarded. They got behind on the house payments. They lived in a Jim Walter house my mother helped her get about 17 years ago. The payments are $220. With the cost of medicine and other bills they were about to lose the house. I wrote the company, told them the story, and they said I could pay the back payments $30.11 a month. I am to pay the regular amount each month and the extra. I stopped being her payee and since they do not read or write they could not stretch the money. Just out of curiosity I ask Jim Walter Company how long she owed on the house. They said 52 months. I went over and told her what the deal was and the $545 income each month was going to have to have the added burden of another $30.11 added, and we had to do this to catch up. She was very cast down. I said "Ida Mae nothing is as bad as what we have come through already. All the children to feed after your husband died and trying to hold on to the house." Her first husband was killed while working in the woods. I said, "Besides you only owe 52 more payments." She has no idea how many years 52 months is but when I got it down to months she jumped up and hugged me and almost lifted me off the ground. She cried and shouted and said "I can hang on, yes I can."

The case of the ----- is improving. This family moved often. They cannot tell you where they have lived. The two oldest children are Indian children, and one is retarded. A neighbor called and told me the family had moved into a shack on her street and had not eaten in five days. I went to see them about three months ago. The conditions were terrible. The man collected scrap, motors, etc. He stayed out of gas for his truck most of the time. The food stamp people would not issue stamps because he did not know what he made or could report satisfactorily. There was no utilities on, rats, cockroaches, flies were about to carry off the house with the family intact. Being from Utah they had never heard of JoAnn Cayce. I have been a long time building trust. One thing the children could understand is food, clothes, tennis shoes and a little love and cold Cokes. Every time they come here I have cold pop. Without an ice box they have starved this summer for cold stuff, but this winter they will starve for hot stuff. They are in school now, and the little four-year-old is in Head Start. We had a time getting a birth certificate. When they can't remember when and where a beautiful little blond, blue eyed, lice-infested four-year-old was born, it hurts. I took my grandson down there with me to carry some toys and some food someone gave me. This child was grabbing and pushing as Daniel tried to help me carry things in. My daughter (who has been fighting cancer treatment and heart failure complications) pulled him to her and said "Daniel is bringing you something. He is not going to take your cars and things. He loves you, and he brought you some of his things." I watched her work a miracle on a little yelling young'un who has had to fight for every bite of food, and he has never had a toy of his own, I don't think. About an hour later we had moved things in, filled out papers, and took care of lots of questions. As we started to go get in the car this little boy said to Daniel "I want you to have this," and he gave him one of the little McDonald cars you get free when you buy a burger. Of course Daniel didn't know what to do, but his mother said "Take it, Daniel, he is your friend and he wants to give you a little car." You could see his little chest swell. "I am giving it to you," he said. Joannie and I had a good cry when we got in the car.

We finally got the little boy his glass eye. I went up with him and watched them make it! He was so happy! Took all day but it looks so real and we did get it in time for the first day of school. This is the little boy I found while looking for someone else. When I saw a rag wrapped around his head I ask to see his mother. Found out when he was 6 he had gotten his eye shot out with a toy bow and arrow. He got one "free eye" at Children's Hospital but one free one was all he could get. So when that one got too small and kept coming out and rolling down the aisle at school his mother put a cloth around his head that covered the eye. I never saw a little boy change so. Before he got his new eye he had been trying to kill himself by sniffing gas. That was a cry for help if I ever heard one. No more "gas" problems now.

We have a ten month old little baby girl born in terrible poverty. They have three babies older. The daddy works in the woods, and mother is in her 20s. This little thing has no bladder opening or a rectum. The tubes are not kept clean and keep coming out. We have to rush this baby back and forth to Children's Hospital. The last time they said they were not letting it come home until there was electricity, a fan, a refrigerator, water and a baby bed. We got all these things and moved them into another house. Things are still bad. They are about to be evicted. The rent is $250. The daddy makes so little and there is much the baby needs that is not covered. The rest of the children have no clothes. I went up before school started, and you would have thought we were having a road-side sale. I spread things out on the trunk of my car, and the mother "shopped." There is a registered nurse and her husband who want to adopt this baby. They have four others who are disabled, and this is how they spend their life. Human Services won't take the baby. This couple will be foster parents to the child or keep it without a check. Of course I don't know what is best, but the baby is going to die, and, in the meantime, it is suffering. The baby is black, the couple wanting to adopt or foster care is white. They have babies of several races and one they feed around the clock every two hours.

Everyday is filled with rounds – I have more calls than I can get to. Many come to the house. I also fill out many papers. I fight the system on everything from a house loan that was approved 18 months ago (and never came through and the tons of paper work I did for the family which can't even be found). We have worked on this for over four years. They live in a shack. I got a boy to help put plastic over the entire top of the house because the rain comes in. We nailed it down under the eaves. This will last about three or four months. A mother, disabled father, and four children live inside and one grandchild born to a 16-year-old mother who died delivering the retarded child.

There is some good news about Evanlyn and Otis. If you remember she is the lady who only had an income of $53 worth of food stamps a month, living in a shack (literally), but we got her in the Pine Cove (nice) apartments. She has to pick up cans for her electricity bill. She eats beans, rice and macaroni. She had a huge tumor in her stomach that a doctor in Pine Bluff said she had to learn to live with. When they brought her to me it was huge and so was she. We had the tumor removed non-cancer, and filed for her SSI (she is slightly retarded). Otis was the starving man who was so crippled and thin I thought he would not live to get off my deck behind my office. It has been a long fight, but Evanlyn has been approved -- but no check yet. Otis got on. He got $7,000 for the first check. They paid back since I had filed. He is the first person who ever gave me money for getting disability for them. I was fixing to leave to take my daughter to M. D. Anderson Institute in Houston, Texas. He knocked on my door. He fell into my arms crying. He had gotten his check, and cashed it at the bank. His sister brought him here. He handed me five $100 bills. I said, "No, you need every penny to fix up that old shack your father left you so you will have a place to live that is warm." He would not have it any other way. I said, "Otis, I am about to leave with my daughter for Houston to a big hospital, her money is very short, and I have helped so many lately mine is short." I said, "I will take it with the understanding you are paying the expense, gas and motel and eats, for us to go to Houston for a week of tests, etc." He grabbed me again and said, "Mrs. Cayce I knew you would do something good with it." He has been able to get glasses, medication, clothes, shoes for his arthritis crippled feet, fix up the house, food in cabinets, get his yard mowed, the old fence removed and even has a used trailer in the yard he is renting to someone cheap who needed a place. If you remember this is the man who touched the CBS men when they saw how thin he was and his circumstances of life. They were here to spend a day in my life. I have kept this man alive with biscuits and sausage from a deli that gave me a sack full three or four times a week. (In the evening when they knew they would not sell them.) I am still carrying Evanlyn things, that are not starches, and maybe her check will come in any day. She has been "examined" by Human Services because they thought, I suppose, I was giving her cash. I guess if I had they would have stopped the $53 worth of stamps. I wish I had time, I would protest, though I hate protestors, and force them to change the name from Human Services to Self-Services. I sometimes think when they changed the name from Welfare Office to Human Service Office they missed the boat. It should be Services for Humans. But they work for the system and the cutbacks and not the human in need. My own daughter who is in the "business" will tell you that. The interest of most are gone, she admits. She said, however, the paper work takes that away. They have no time for people because of the paper work involved. I fight that also.

Remember Randy? He had TB, and I got him a place with a widow and he has been so bad. I noticed that his legs were not right and found he had a tumor on his spine that was paralyzing him. Well, he had surgery, got his disability, married the widow, remodeled her house (all her kids then moved in), and his life will be perfect when he gets his Medicare card. His TB is testing clear. He comes to see me and just looks at me and cries. He still can't believe he got through all those months of pain and starvation and homelessness. I told him he doesn't have the Grace now. It is gone because he doesn't need it for those troubles. He now believes "my grace is sufficient."

There are many things I would like to tell you about. Juneus is one. He was talking "funny," hardly whispering. He told me the day I went over to see his 80-year-old mother who had a bad hip that he had a sore throat. I ask how long and he said since December, which was four months before. I said, "Juneus you do not have a sore throat. I think you are in trouble." He smoked. His troubles were mine because he had lost his job and had no insurance or income. I took him to the throat people at the University Hospital and to make a short story they operated and found cancer in the voice box and throat and spread farther, they said, than they hoped before surgery. The task of finding him a place to stay in Little Rock during the week, taking him every Monday and going for him every Friday and feeding him while he was up there was something I really strained to do, but it was something, like most things, there is no turning back. When you start CPR you have to keep pumping until all life is gone or the ambulance gets there. So we have finished the radiation for 8 weeks, and he is home with his mother. He has had his disability filed for him, and I have had the first turn down. The Social Security folks keep me in hot water filling out papers time and time again. They know me, and I think sometimes they surely know I don't have time to file for folks riding the system. I wonder why they do this to my cases. Some take 18 months to two years, and I have a person without any means that I have to take on to care for and keep alive until the check starts. Some have died before it got here. Some give up waiting and trying to cope without medication, and tell me "Mrs. Cayce, let me die. You can't do no more."

Right now I have a family with five children who have head lice and body lice; the father got a job and is walking nine miles one way to work. But they have no money for food or head lice treatment. My son wants me to see about this family tomorrow before I leave to go to Pennsylvania. They also need food and lights on, and above all water turned on. The father will get his first check next week.

I want to feed folks Thanksgiving, the poor, elderly and disabled eat with us. Thanksgiving is a time folks need folks. I need money and food to do this. We fed over 600 last Thanksgiving. I also need to get started washing, dressing and "wigging" my used dolls for Christmas and collecting toys, books, etc. I have many who need medicine, lights, water, food, children who need shoes. I had a big clothes give-away Friday, Sept. 11th. We gave away over 10,000 pounds of used clothing. It took me a week to move it to the Armory and sort it. Then I took the "leftovers" to Arkadelphia to the Bee Hive for the retarded to have and sell the buttons, etc., nothing is wasted. Thank each one who not only sent me some donations this year (this averages about $200 a month, and sometimes, if I have something great going, I will have about $300 to work with). I now have my tax-deductible charity set up by a lawyer who worked free. I hope I can get more funds and especially food. My husband is retired now, and I run in the road so much I don't sell as many antiques, so sometimes the needs out here are overwhelming, and I can do nothing about them. Some called me and asked me if I wanted to send a truck load of used clothing to Louisiana to the storm victims. I said, "listen I am fighting a hurricane right here and with a broom stick." I am so sorry this happened. I am sure the needs were great. I know 100% of what I get handed to me gets to the source. I see your dollars and my time and dollars work. I want to tell all of you how much I love you. How I pray for you and thank you for the love and concern you have for others.

I am working on a case of a 15-year-old, who was expelled last week from school for the year. I have to try to find this boy a home and a school that will accept him. It seems that counseling and help should be available for his case. It should not fall into the hands of a volunteer who has no training except to love children. I have known this child since he was born, dropped on a bare floor. His mother had every man in the country around him. The abusive way they treated him would make your hair curl. Then he was away for about eight years and she has gone to prison. He was moved back here. He is mad and blames the world for the insecurity and hardships and hunger and filth he has endured. He will likely cost society for about 20 to 30 years of incarceration in prison. He must be helped now. We have about a year to do this. He is not violent yet just, and I say "just" with great pain – big mouthed and surly. I had him with me at the clothes give-away, and I could see a great change by the end of the day. I touched him every chance I got on the shoulder and said what a good job he was doing. He loved it. I thought probably these were the first kind words he had ever heard. Children are no different from a dog. You teach an animal to be mean by the treatment you give him, and he will either withdraw and wither and die or he will fight everything and everybody. I know the system must surely know this! To put a child, with inner trouble, out on the streets and say the schools do not want you and not offer any help is cruel, and professional people should be ashamed. Amen!

Our Literacy Classes are started, and we can operate for one full year. We have a large group and more calling and asking to come. We have all volunteer teachers, and most of the food is donated. I am only buying the coffee and cokes. I told them I would not help unless we could feed these folks a meal before class, get glasses for those who could not see, child care for the mothers and transportation for all. We were able to get this.

I was at the clothes give-away Friday, 11th, and a ragged man came up to me with terrible scratches on his hands and arms. He wanted to see me outside. I was so busy with about 400 people grabbing clothes and me giving out trash bags and watching children for mothers, but I told him if he were willing to wait I would get to him. He waited, and I went outside to meet with him. I wondered what in the world this big man wanted and where these scratches came from. He told me he "heard" about my school. I told him if he could not read or write we were still accepting people. He started to cry and said, "I want to spell and read and write." (He added spelling.) He said, "When you are in a group, and everyone knows more than you, and someone hands you something to read, you just feel so bad." I started to cry too. He said "I can't come at night." I ask, why? He said "I catches chickens all night." If some of you do not know what this is I will tell you, he goes into the chicken house after the chickens have gone to roost, grabs a handful of broilers then takes them and puts them in a cage and goes back for more. He is smelling this all night. Working in near dark and getting scratches from finger to shoulder and often in the face and eye. It is back breaking but for $3.20 an hour these folks will do it. They have no choice, many of them. Well, that was a challenge for me. He can't come at night, and I have no days left. I did find someone with training in this method to help him and they (actually) need him as much as he needs them. It often works out this way. This depressed person will teach him afternoons before he goes to the chicken houses. I guess the man will sleep mornings.

The world is a strange and wonderful place. I sometimes wish I had time to just "sit a spell," as my granny used to say, and think about it. I have very little "thinking time" and not as much personal time as I actually need to even bathe and sleep. I went out late the other night for sick folks and told my husband I was going to Badland. He said how long would I be gone? I told him I should be back in 30 to 45 minutes. I got back much later and his car was gone. I thought "Oh, my! He is out looking for me." It was about 11:00. Finally he came in, and I said, "I am so sorry, have you been out looking for me? I had to get the child to the hospital." He said, "No, I was at the mayor's house, we were going over some things for the City." (My husband is clerk and treasurer for the City.) For just a minute I was pretty hurt. He had not worried one bit, in fact even forgot I was gone. I went on in the house and started to work up a good "pity party" for myself then I thought, if that man worried about me every time I am out of sight or gone into dangerous places, his life would be miserable and mine surely would be. I then got tickled, ate my supper and went to bed. When he came from his office, I was past caring.

Love to you all!

Remember me, I need you!
JoAnn Cayce

March 18, 1993

Greetings:

It is hard to believe I have not found a moment I felt I had a choice to choose to write you the "news" since September, '92. Each day has its choices, but I find, as has been the case for over forty years, the most serious and helpful things actually "leave me no personal choice." I have to do what I have to do and go on from there. Sometimes I feel God makes my choices. It is a "strange path," oft times, that "leads" to certain people's problems. I know a few who support my causes do not support my faith. I grant you that right, but I have to testify there is overwhelming evidence God delivers many.

I do want to thank each one who gives me a thought, a prayer and/or a donation. The best "nation" you know, is a "donation."

Looking back to September, '92, when I left you in my last "Newsletter" I had a lady at the University Hospital. Her hysterectomy proved she did not have cancer. She was in her late 60s. I think I told you I went to her house to check on her retarded grandchild, and, in questioning her about her blood pressure, found she had constant bleeding and had had for years. I was in a state of panic. Her husband is an invalid; her mother is living and nearly 100 years old. The grandson, (abandoned) is to be cared for also. I thought if this woman has cancer what will become of the family? She now needs a mammogram since she has recently lost a sister to breast cancer. I have found no one who will do this free. Med Center wants $65 in advance. I have about 11 women who need one badly. If anyone wants to sponsor one ($65) I will be happy to furnish the transportation, get the appointment, etc. There is NO FREE program for this. Medicaid won't pay, I understand.

I told you in September little Thomas has his glass eye. Well about that time I heard about a teenager who got her eye put out in school when a boy shot a paper clip with a rubber band. The eye was removed free, but again funds to get a "new eye" have only just now come through for her. I have taken her several times, for fittings etc. This past week she got her "eye." She sat in the front seat with me and her mother and a friend with a year old baby in the back seat. I kept noticing her leaning against the window looking out at what appeared to be the road as we traveled home. Finally it hit me! She was looking at herself in the outside car mirror. I said "Theresa, you are so beautiful with your new eye." She responded, "Yes, I know." I said, "Does it hurt?" She said, "It don't hurt!" I knew it did, they always do for awhile, but she was not taking any chances on giving it back. While I was taking these folks for the glass eye, I took them out to eat at Wendy's. They had the salad bar. They loved it! They could not believe it! I also took them to University Mall one time and to Park Plaza Mall the next time. They walked and looked for two hours. They had no money. When I came back and picked all four up they were so delighted by all they had seen, riding on the escalator and elevator, I knew they could not have had more pleasure if they had had money! It would have only slowed them down in seeing things! Each time I took them they invited the young girl with the baby. At first I thought I was being taken advantage of. Then I realized how unselfish this is. Sometimes those of us who are able to have and do, do not want our "friends" to have, right?

Some of you will want to know about our Literacy Classes. They are going great since September. We have had a few drop-outs but those who are faithful are so happy to be able to write more than just their names. Some who could read and write limited are "part time" instructors now for others. The things I insisted we have – food, transportation, childcare – have worked beautifully.

Some of you will want to know about our birth control and Norplant program. Things are improving, but we need to get out more information to those who do not read. Every conception we prevent with teenagers is a strike against misery for both mother and child and saving the system funds for better things like health care!

A caller called long distance who "heard" about me and ask me how much "moral" teaching I was doing about sexual abstinence. I told him with feeding the hungry, doctoring the sick, clothing the unclothed, filling out papers for the disabled and watching out for the elderly, retarded, disabled, children at risk, abused children, battered women, my "prisoner program," literacy, trying to make a living and helping my husband in his ministry, work and projects I had little time left. I ask him if he wanted to come do the job I would be happy to give him maps to the areas, names of families he could start with. He hung up!

November, 1992, was filled from can to can't. I look back at my calendar and wonder how I kept it all going! Not really. Determination and refusal to accept defeat, teamed with total commitment to each project, little victories each day, one step at a time keeps me going always. I tell you this because this is the most asked question, how do I keep going. I had personal problems, migraines almost daily, and then I moved my daughter and her five-year-old home with us the 31st of October. Her furniture, rubble of a 15 year marriage, his constant threats, our changing all our locks, made me understand and appreciate other's problems. But we cannot allow our personal problems of health or family to interfere with our helping others. We have tools such as education, money, food, shelter, and the people I find or find me, have no tools. I run into walls, in some cases, that seem impossible to scale. It is a "walk through" in most every case. In some I have to carry people sometimes the whole family. Sometimes besides being poor these people are also sick, crippled, mentally ill, addicts, cold, hungry, illiterate and often even unwilling to change to save themselves or their children. They have so little faith, or hope things will ever be any better. In some cases they chose rather to die. I simply cannot let them do this.

Back to November, I had hearings in Federal Court for some disabled whose appeals with Social Security had reached that point. I took some to the University Out-Patient Clinic. One was Willie, who had a serious back injury. Also he and his wife woke up and found the youngest of their six children dead in bed between them.

The day we were in the waiting room waiting for the doctor to come in, Willie leaned over to me and said, "Mrs. Cayce I am going to kill myself." He said it like he would say, "Mrs. Cayce it is starting to rain outside." I tried to be calm and said the silliest thing "When?" He said, "I am thinking about it now." I said, "Don't move until I get back." I went out the door, grabbed the first nurse and said, "This man I brought says he is going to kill himself." Needless to say, in minutes the room was full. Most know me and often say I bring them some of the worst cases. Willie ended up at the State Hospital that day with no clothes, crying in my arms, begging me to tell his wife, see to his children and saying he didn't want to be locked up. The two weeks in State Hospital was the best thing that has happened to Willie. It got him a "record" of mental troubles that allowed me to get him on disability! I maybe never could have with his back injury. He, his children and wife are now getting a Social Security check. They have a little house, running water, and a bathroom for the first time! They have food, shoes, and beds, and most important to them, their deceased 9-month-old has a head stone. This family taught me so much. I have lots of it filed away. I learned to ask a child, "Why are you walking crippled?" because of one of Willie's children. I went to see about them, and their child was running around but walked "funny." I usually see children limping and never say a word, but I did that day. He said, "I stuck a nail in my foot." I said, "When?" Come to find out, it was the last day a tetanus shot would have done any good! It showed signs, the Children's Hospital said, of being "hot for tetanus." They started treatment that day.

November was also the month for gathering food for the annual Thanksgiving Dinner. I had no time to get a letter out and ask you for help in financing this, but Jan came to my rescue in Virginia and asked Tyson for hens. They gave me 100. A Cable Company gave me 13 turkeys, and others donated enough to number 25. I put a box at the Antique Shop for peas, corn, beans, and the Methodist Church at Fordyce gave me a big boost helping buy napkins, plates, cups, potatoes, coffee, 100 dozen eggs. The Caring Institute that awarded me the National Award for one of the ten Most Caring persons in America, gave me milk. We fed 808 persons Thanksgiving Day. We started about 4:00 a.m., and the volunteers drifted in all day – just enough. I know there was a higher power working because no way could I have cooked for so many. I had cooked the 100 hens in my yard and kitchen on Tuesday with the help of my son and a total stranger who called and said, "I heard about your effort to feed the poor on Thanksgiving, can I help?" I said, "Can you start now?" She came in, introduced herself while I tied an apron around her middle. We took chicken off the bone until late. She also baked corn bread.

Having the School Cafeteria was a miracle! I have always cooked at the Armory under almost primitive conditions – small ovens that won't work, one sink, one ice box (home type) etc. At the school they had "everything!" Modern equipment, beaters, huge pots, sinks, hot servers, huge stoves, you name it – it was like the meal was prepared in heaven. The school furnished the dietician to help. She did the "bossing" and I followed. It was wonderful! About 10:00 a.m. the street people, walking poor, homeless started coming in. It was an hour before we were to start serving but we gave them hot coffee. Seeing them seated in the beautifully decorated dining hall (compliments of Dallas County Hospital staff) shivering from the very cold day, set us on fire to make it the best and prettiest meal they had ever eaten. All my family came to help. Some in-laws came from Tennessee. One lady heard about this event and flew in from Virginia. Professional people helped, common people, church people, and some came from surrounding towns and gave from two to six hours. We made all the trimmings and had deserts (furnished by Klappenbach Bakery). Roxanne and Dennis Daniels (Camden) had had a spuds party and peeled and baked four bushels of candied sweet potatoes, furnished by the Stones of Eagle Mill, delivered them and stayed all day working. We had over 600 pounds of dressing, 25 smoked-to-perfection turkeys, 100 gallons giblet gravy, creamed potatoes, sweet potatoes, cranberries, peas, corn, string beans, tea, coffee, milk, bread. We delivered about two hundred plates to the elderly, disabled, and families who could not come in. We served the jails and inmates wrote letters of thanks. It was truly a wonderful Thanksgiving! The next day when we had our personal Thanksgiving here at the house and cooked steaks outside, we recounted little children stuffing food in and some who tired to hid things for later. Especially touching was the woman who stole a bag filled with cartons of milk. A mother who has to steal to feed her children in America proves something is wrong with the system.

I want to tell you this family's story: They moved to Fordyce, Arkansas, October, 1992. I did not hear about them until Christmas. A Social Service person called me before Christmas Eve. She told me this family would have no Christmas, said they were "new in town." She said they had no transportation; there were eight small children and a grandfather. I told her to bring them down. "They came for food and toys. I ask the worker why these folks were hungry. She said, "They do not have Social Security cards or birth certificates for the children, so they can't get food stamps." But she said, "They are getting them, and we will soon be able to help them." I gave them our own Christmas turkey, ham and all the canned goods that had been left at our door. I also had sugar, meal, flour, beans Sherwood Clinic had brought me. I had not distributed it all. There was this grandfather and lots of children. I asked him why he had moved from Chicago here and with no information. He said he had lost all his own children to the streets of Chicago. He said he and his wife were going to raise these children, but she died. He said he knew he had no chance if he stayed in Chicago, so he moved back near where he was born with all the grandchildren. He is 71-years-old. One of the older granddaughters has a four-year-old child which is also here. There are 13 in all living in the house. I gave them warm clothes, toys and the food. I forgot these folks because the Human Service worker said everything was going to work out for them soon. This was the 22nd of December. Two weeks ago about March first, I ran into this Social Worker and asked her, "How is the ----- family doing?" Her answer knocked me over. She said, "Mrs. Cayce you ought to go over there, it is so pitiful." I said, "Are they sick, or what?" She said, "They still ain't got (her words) no help – they is hungry, cold and about lost all hope." I had my day planned but my plans are always subject to change. She told me where they lived, over by the back gate of the cemetery. I thought after I found all the story out that the location is very fitting! They lived in a big old open house. I had to remind the grandfather who I was, and when I did, he started crying and grinning. I said, "Why haven't you told that Social Worker to call Mrs. Cayce?" He said, "I don't know?" The house was freezing cold. I said, "Is there no heat?" He said there had not been any all winter. I said I did not know Christmas you had no heat. He said he did not have lights either at Christmas, but since then he got a Social Security check and got on lights. He gets $435 a month. He pays $150 for the shack of a house, and his light bill had been $269 that month. He did not know why. We still have not been able to figure that out. There were children everywhere. They looked like a birthday party in the slums. The 17-year-old with the baby had every thing very clean. No working bathroom and no hot water but everything was scrubbed. I went through the house. Not only was there no heat, but the beds (such as they were) were almost bare – no cover, just ragged sheets and two had a little ragged pad. The ice box was small and bare. The children were looking at me with big eyes. I went to Wal-Mart for a big electric heater. (Betty Arhens had mailed me $100 that day.) I got other things and went back. I went home and started gathering things I had: blankets, bedding, food, soap, toilet tissue, and called the Methodist Church secretary, Jo Trussell. She gave me a check for $50 from emergency funds. I got fruit, among other things, and when I saw the five-and-four-year-old grab an orange I almost lost control. I had taken my daughter (who had moved in with us on Halloween) to see three of the children I thought were mentally retarded (she agreed). This is my daughter who is in heart failure from treatment of cancer on her heart so she could not stay long in that cold. I stayed, trying to get names, birth dates, feeding them and working with the 17-year-old. Found the old man was sick and no one had Medicaid cards. It has been two weeks and a never ending job with this family. I have accomplished much and in only one day I called a plumber, and he told me Human Services had called him in October, 1992, and wanted him to check the gas lines and see if it were safe to turn the gas on. He did and called them within hours and told them it was safe. I found no one will acknowledge the plumber talked to them. The gas was never turned on, and this family has gone through the four hardest months of winter (Nov., Dec. Jan. & Feb.) with no heat! The income has gone for electricity and rent! This family has been hungry, cold and without hope all winter.

The children could not get free lunches because they had no Social Security cards and birth certificates. I could not find anyone working on this at all. In fact, I was told the case was about to be closed out at the Welfare office. When there is paper work that stands between a hungry child and food, that is too much paper work. There should be something out here in the way of emergency help between rules and food besides JoAnn Cayce. If this can happen to this family it can (and does) happen to families all over Arkansas and maybe other states. The frustration of this case the last two weeks would try Job. You who have sent me $10 to $25 lately have helped this family get heat, hot water, bathroom fixed, food and the breakfast and lunch program. Thank you! I have made many calls back and forth to Chicago, Social Security, and the Social Security numbers were "dug" out of the system. Some birthdays we did not know. Some "real" names the grandfather did not know. Names like Pumpkin, Penny, Puddin had become "real" names. One mother of one bunch of these children I found died of an overdose at 29 in Chicago. One bunch has a mother in Chicago who is still having children. Has a one-, two-, and four-year-old. God only knows what condition these children are in. I tried to talk to this mother on the phone. She is totally unresponsive. The grandfather seems to be a fine man. He has been a janitor. He is dense, but he had given up hope and did not know if help would ever come. There are three retarded children. I need bedding, towels, dishes, children's clothes, food, toys, books, light bulbs, and glasses for the grandfather. There are many families such as this one. I want to get this family on the programs, be payee for the retarded three boys, move them to a decent house, and get the 15-year-old in school. The school system won't accept him (remember, been 5 months now) because he doesn't have a transcript. Seems no one is trying to get one and the boy is walking dynamite! Walking around in rags, hungry and with nothing to do, cold and on the street.

One young man is getting out of college soon that I have gone to their house and kept them fed for years. His disabled father died last year from untreated diabetes. I kept him in insulin, and he was approved after four years of fighting for disability (he worked at Georgia-Pacific for 21 years) the week before he died. Never drew a check. This kid hugged me the other day and said, "Mrs. Cayce, I appreciate the food, clothes, and encouragement growing up but what I appreciated the most was you keeping my father in medication and you kept fighting his disability case. He died knowing he was going to start getting checks."

I must tell you about Christmas and let you go.

I started collecting toys as soon as Christmas was over last Christmas and had many used toys, most very greatly used. The first of December, 1992, I put the word out to those with children and means that I wanted all their used toys. I wrote KSSN in Little Rock who, along with Bob Robbins, Mike and the gang, and Jerry Atchley (owner of the station), always support my Christmas cause.

My husband and I went up to KSSN to get the things they had collected, and we also picked up a generous check. We went straight to Wal-Mart, Kmart, Fred's, KaBees and other budget toy stores and spent what they gave us and what we had to put with it. We came home with a truck filled with "Santa." The names were pouring in – schools, churches, teachers, Human Services, families and the families we had been working with came to a grand total of 425 children. We filled bags for the children, also stockings of fruit, candy and had the help of Dallas County Hospital staff working on the stockings (we took all the supplies to them and they did the work). They did a beautiful job. Families picked up at the Armory and then the "fun" started. From the 20th to the 27th emergencies and families with no Christmas, burnt out families, families who had serious problems came. It was the strangest thing someone would call they had no food or knew a family with no food, and I would look out on the porch and there would be a box of food. This happened over and over for about four days. Even our own small grandchildren fixed Christmas for other children. They never questioned why Santa did not come to see them. They just shared their own toys and gathered from the collection left. Toys continually being brought in until every family and child was taken care of.

The second of December our family flew to Washington, D. C. for me to accept the National Caring Award from the Hall of Fame Caring Institute. It was awarded in the Senate Caucus Room where the Anita Hill and Clarence Thomas hearings were held and the Watergate hearings were also there many years ago. Gay, Frank and little Cayce did not get to go, but all the rest of our children and their children went. With Hartsel and me, there were ten of us. American Airlines helped with the tickets. The Marriott Hotels furnished most of the beautiful rooms and meals. Senators David Pryor, and Dale Bumpers furnished tours and dinners, and celebrations went on for four days. The day the awards were presented in the Senate Room, it was packed with people and reporters. The Editor of Reader's Digest introduced me, and as I walked to the podium I crumpled the outline for my speech and put it in the pocket of my suit. I had made my decision two minutes before. I had been sitting on stage looking at the crowd. I thought, looking out at the bright television lights, if I don't tell Washington what it is like to be poor and have to live by rules made by educated folks who never walked the road, they will never know. In a few minutes I tried to touch the heart of each one. It was quiet an experience because as soon as I finished I could not have told you what I said, but the crowd rushed me and my own family could not get to me.

I want to thank each one of you for listening to this rapid report. I want to tell you I love you. If I don't hear from you, that is fine, I know you are there. If you have anything used, for home, or body, drop it off on my porch, or take it to Kandy and Ted in Little Rock (Phone number 835-3013) or to Gay and Frank Buttrey in Arkadelphia (246-7376). Joannie is no longer living in Little Rock and is here with us. She is happy here. She recently experienced her first clothes give-away in many years. They have grown considerably, and she was shocked beyond words. All I ask for is household goods and clothes families no longer need. Allow me to recycle them to others whose lives will be improved. Unlike Goodwill and Salvation Army I give this away totally without charge.

Much love, sincerely,
JoAnn Cayce

December 8, 1993

Dear Friends,

I cannot remember when I have mailed you a written report of the happenings around here. I start one sometimes, and the phone rings, and I'm off. I think about many things, when they happen, and I promise myself that when I write my friends who support me with love and charity, I am going to tell them about this because they deserve to know. If it is uplifting or funny I especially want you to know.

The night of December 5th, I came in from Washington D.C. and while in Washington I determined to try to get the word out to others of the great need there is in this country for us to be concerned about the pain there is in poverty. I am told often, by folks who claim to know, that I see more "raw" poverty at the source of its existence than any social worker today. I suppose because most social workers see the poor who come to their office, and they usually try to look presentable. When you go to the homes and see the conditions there, it is so much different. If you have concern in your heart for others, it plain hurts.

I went to Washington on invitation from the National Caring Hall of Fame for Caring Americans. After hearing the experiences and suffering going on, not only in America, but in foreign countries to help folks cope with poverty, I am again renewed that nothing I can do is too much when it relieves the suffering of a human being.

We had just finished our Thanksgiving Dinner when I left for Washington. I kept remembering the little boy whose family came, and while the mother and daddy waited in a line on each side of the table, this little boy waited on himself. He came back and back to the serving line asking for 1/2 pints of milk until he had drunk 9 cartons. He also ate seconds of Thanksgiving Dinner, and his big eyes seemed afraid each time he came back that he would be turned away. I had to get in a tiny little corner of that School Cafeteria and wipe the tears of thankfulness to God for the blessing of being able to take the funds others gave me and prepare the meal. Volunteers helped me put the pain of hunger away for awhile. Some families have to choose between selling their food stamps and paying the electricity bill or eating in the dark. Food stamps are not designed to feed a family totally to begin with. If a home manager has the education and wit to manage, they can shop sales etc. and maybe feed a family for 18 to 20 days out of the month. You and I know many poor cannot read, do not have transportation to go to the cheaper stores, and have very little managing ability. Of course I sometimes see drugs, alcohol and abuse of the stamps and children's aid and this makes for even more hungry children.

We had a little boy at one of the feeding sites this summer who ate 9 breakfasts each of the first two mornings he was there. After that it dropped each morning until he was eating 3 each day. I was told it never fell below that. This is America, and it breaks my heart, with all the waste in this country, children have to go to bed with the toothache, earache, tummy ache and many sleep on the floor. Sometimes there is violence in the home, lots of noise, yelling, no instruction, and concern for rules or teaching any principles. It is no wonder we have as much crime! I helped a 14-year-old male last year when he was expelled from school and helped get him into another school. I talked to him all year, stuck close and kept telling him how, starting anew, he could do it! He had the chance of a lifetime because with changing school he did not have to live up to the bad that was expected of him. He made almost straight As and Bs at the new school, and this year he is back at his "old" school and doing great! The counselor said he did not know what happened! I had to tell him what this boy told me Thanksgiving Day. He had come to volunteer and stayed to mop the floor. He said, "Mrs. Cayce, you told me I could last year, and no one else had ever told me that before." I said, "Was I right?" He said "Yes." I said, "Then you never let me or yourself down!"

Today I had a family come for help where the father was hurt in an accident on the job. He is totally disabled, and his Worker's Comp has been cut off. He has filed for Social Security Disability but it may be months or several years before he gets any income coming into the home. He has never been on the system before and doesn't have the least idea how to get food stamps or help. His wife must take care of him and a four-year-old while a 7-, and 9-year-old go to school. His children are looking under the Christmas tree and asking if they will get anything for Christmas, and someone told the parents about me. He said he had a nice house but had no gas for the butane tank. He wife said she could cut wood if she could get a power saw. I ask him if she had ever cut wood before. He broke and said she had never had too. This father is in his 30's. When I think of all he has to learn about the system and how slow the wheels turn and how poverty stricken you have to be to get any relief and how little it is I weep, for the pain there is in the future of this family before any real help ever comes. I just hope they are a strong family, or they will not survive. Some fathers commit suicide before there is an improvement. One father who was injured in an automobile accident last year was in this condition except he had four little girls. At first he lay and combed the children's hair and cried a little but as the food got shorter and situation grew worse and worse and he had no insurance, medication or a doctor who would continue on his case free (he was crushed from the waist down), he gave up. He could not walk, it was Christmas then too. He started asking me questions like, "Mrs. Cayce, if I died would my wife and children get Social Security?" I finally said, "What are you thinking about, maybe that a cheap funeral is the way out?" He leaned on his pillow and said, "Do you have anything better to tell me about?" I started yelling and then I went out and cried all the way home.

It is not easy out here. I know there is no time for tears but sometimes they come anyway. I called several this morning, some young and with a good start in a business or job. I ask them about cutting some wood for this family so the little children might be warm and three times I was told, "Mrs. Cayce, I would love to help you, and I do have a power saw, but I am so busy." These same fellows would say (if the daddy commits suicide) "You know looks like someone could have helped that guy. What could have brought him to that?"

It is within the power of all of us to do something. It should not be within any of us to say "I am too busy." God has a way of showing

folks who think they are too busy to help their fellow man to slow
down a little and let their blessings catch up, and maybe they will
improve a little with the knowledge "life doesn't owe them a thing!"

It is time to get out all the used toys I have been putting away
and try to do some "doll dressing and hair combing," a little make-up
and "think up." I hope to get candy, fruit, shoes, sweaters, a few ball
gloves, balls, games, and about 100 good children's coats. If you find
you have grandchildren's toys laying around or children's clothes,
shoes, sweaters gather them up and get them to me or my daughter
in Arkadelphia (246-7376) or to Kandy in Little Rock (835-3013).
They will be happy to get them to me. Of course my porch is always
a welcome place for any kind of drop-offs (except dogs and cats).
Some folks have been putting them out and I won't let them go
hungry but really am not running a kennel.

I always need medication for some, shoes for folks, need blankets
this time of the year, need groceries all the time for families. I can
sure use beds, dressers, chests, towels (those old thin ones and sheets
you don't want or need). I had a little child snuggle up to me the
other day. I felt him quiver with fear and cold. I wondered what
folks do who have never felt the weight of being needed so greatly!
To me it is the thing that keeps me head and shoulders above despair,
depression, greed, unthankfulness and unloving thoughts. I won't say
I do not have faults but knowing things can get very bad, very fast,
with no possible solution available changes things. I see families who
are so desperate, and sometimes I have no finances to help them. But
they know I am there for them and trying to find a way out of the
maze.

A man came by with a bad toe and a little problem and wondered
where he could get some salve for a sore toe. I knew that look and
would never have let him leave without seeing that toe. It almost
came off in his sock. My daughter who, with her five year old lives
with me now, was called into the room. She is a registered nurse. I
had a medical opinion without shock. She said he had to have help
at once or possibly lose his foot. She got on the phone calling friends
of hers at the University Hospital. She is unable to work anymore,
but she still has connections. After we had gotten help and surgery
for that man he came back later to thank us. I knew we would never
see him again. He is a poor working man with no insurance but he

was a proud man. The knowledge God led him here and we were able to help him, lifted my heart to the hills, but the humbleness I felt God cared about his toe so much He wanted him to keep it and sent him to us, and we were a tool in saving the toe really humbled us. It is a wonder someone is not out here fighting for my job. Nothing is more fulfilling and the overtime is always available.

One night sometime back my phone rang and I answered, and a woman started crying and telling me how badly her teeth hurt. She said they were rotted off even with her gums. She was 62 and not drawing anything but food stamps. She had no place to live, and folks just sorta kept her for a time and she moved on. She lived mostly on starches and said the pain in her teeth never went away. I could feel her misery over the phone. I hate pain like this. It is an enemy I fight all the time. There is a sound it makes like nothing I can describe, but over a period of forty some odd years, I recognize it as my enemy. I told her I had no money to get her teeth fixed and even if I were able to get her on Medicaid (which is doubtful), they still do not fix teeth – not even children's teeth. I told her I had no dentist who would work on her teeth around here, but I may could beg a doctor in Little Rock to ease her pain. I would call and for her to get back to me. She had no phone of course and was at a neighbor's. I started to hang up, and she said, "Mrs. Cayce, if you can't get someone to pull my teeth I am going to get out here on these streets and make me some money like these other girls and get my teeth pulled." She said she was a Christian woman but could not stand the pain any longer. I have used humor many times to stop tears. I said laughing, "Sara you stay home nights because you are a year older than me and I could not earn a dime out on the streets. We are over the hill." She laughed, and I promised help. So you see my problems are of a variety out here that knows no bounds or classes. A dog may be brought here with a collar embedded in it's neck or like the other night I was out long after dark putting straw, scrap sheet rock inside a dog house of a poor family. I had gone by and watched that dog freezing for about three weeks. One day I went up in the alley to feed the alcoholics, and as I went by that dog, I said, "Dog, I don't know your name but before I go to bed tonight I am going to see that you are out of that mud hole and in a warm place to sleep, or I will not go to bed." I did not get up there until about 9 or 10 that night but that dog was waiting as if he understood the promise. It was standing up in the mud waiting. When I left he was full and huddling in the warmness of not only insulation, straw, leaves and hay but he had felt the pats of love and words. I feel he will remember the visit a long time. In fact, when I finished telling the lady how much her dog deserved a better place, and if he could bark and scare danger away and be such a friend to her, the least she could do is get him a pan to eat out of instead of off the muddy ground. Surely she could keep something in his house and keep it moved where there was no mud and pat and talk to him some each day since she had absolutely nothing to do. She seemed to look at the dog with some respect in the lights of my truck as I left. She may have just really seen that dog for the first time. I did notice today he has a pan now! He doesn't seem to be hunting something around his house. Makes me think his stomach is more acquainted with something besides air. Oh! to care ... to care ... it feels so good!

I love all my friends and thank each one who continues to believe in me and my causes.

Merry Christmas to you and yours! Truly the needs of others are everyone's burden. We are our brother's keeper! As my 5-year-old grandson said, "Granny, what if I were poor?"

What if you were poor? Truly needy, who would care?

Sincerely,

JoAnn Cayce

November 1, 1994

Dear Wonderful Friends,

I can't remember the last time I mailed out a news (Charity) letter. I think it was in May, 1994. I can't believe 1994 has flown so fast but when I stop and think of all that has been accomplished I do not regret the year has gone. It has been one when some have improved. Many can look back and say "only by the grace of God did we survive."

I was working in a very poor area this week, had been in a terrible hurry because I am getting a clothes give-away ready to be November 4th. I will have to be honest; I was a little put out that I had to even go because of the time. I stopped at the house, the lady was so poor. I noticed the clean yard and humble plants. Then I looked on the porch. I was touched to the quick and eyes filled with tears. She had a commode sitting on the porch without the tank, just sitting there like a vase, free standing. It was filled with beautiful growing flowers of all colors. She was using the old commode from the nearby City Dump for a flower pot. I took care of my business, promised to make arrangements for her medication needed so badly, and explained why I thought the boil on the son's back kept coming back, told them why I thought the lights would burn on one side of the house and would not burn on the other side. I promised to try to find some soft number 12 shoes for the son (he is 46 and retarded). As I left I again had a long look at the commode filled with sweet smelling impatiens, petunias and even a morning glory vine. I thought about the little saying "it is better to light a candle than curse the darkness" – here is a lady who lights a little candle in her own way. Perhaps she never owned a candle, but in her humble way she lights one instead of cursing the problems life has handed her.

So much has happened you deserve to hear about, know about and rejoice with me in. Many things have happened that you could get a great lesson from and some things you would surely appreciate. Some you would laugh about!

November 2, 1994

Yesterday I left the Armory after sorting clothes all day. I told the lady I had hired to help me "I am going home, fix my husband a bite (he had had nothing to eat all day) and go to bed. I told her I had been up since 3:00 a.m. But instead I went home and on my porch sat a man who looked like a whipped puppy.

I moved this man to another town some months ago because there was no housing space for him here. I could get him into a housing complex and his rent subsidized. He is retarded and alone. He reported drug activity a few weeks ago and was shot because of this. He wanted to move back here where he was "safe" closer to me. He moved into a shack without me knowing it. He had no utilities, heat, bedding, furniture, food, but he was here on my porch late in the evening depending on me to make everything right. I felt like I could not pull my own stairs but James and I went into the attic, drug him out a mattress. I got sheets, pillows and cases. Found him some dishes, pots and pans, some other necessities and took him home. It was dark by the time we set up things and arranged for utilities, etc. A little stray puppy had taken up on his porch, and James was so proud of it. I wondered why? Here is a man who can not feed himself, yet he rejoiced over a starving puppy. I thought the dog could not find a worse home! As I walked to the truck he took the puppy up in his arms and with loving licks and tail wagging I realized they needed each other – they may starve but they would not suffer because they were "alone." I thought "will I never learn?"

November 3, 1994

Today I am looking for baby clothes for a little infant boy. He is wanted but is naked and born to a little couple who have no manger or swaddling clothes to wrap him in. I need baby clothes badly.

I am looking for panties for a little eight year old who is wearing men's underwear to school and the children are laughing at her. I need children's clothes badly.

I need to get the gas turned on for a man who is bedfast because of his 4th surgery. He cannot get out of bed and has no heat. He and his 14-year-old daughter are alone and four months behind in the rent.

I am trying to plan the Thanksgiving Dinner which is to be the 24th and it is the 3rd. I expect to feed 1,000 or more. I need hams, turkeys, canned goods, meal, onions, celery, eggs, sugar, spices, oleo, instant potatoes, to the tune of enough to feed 1,000. We feed the elderly, homeless, disabled, mothers, fathers, and hungry children, folks in transit, in situations they cannot help. If families who are working and getting a few food stamps or those unemployed who live only on food stamps spend what they get for a big Thanksgiving dinner they have to do without all the rest of the month. We encourage them to come eat with us so they will have food all month. We would love to have milk if possible especially for the elderly and children. They can drink water and/or Kool-Aid if necessary. I would like for everyone to have a piece of ham and a slice of turkey. We fixed over 650 pounds of dressing last year, southern style, with gravy on top. We feed the men in jails. This is one thing I am strong about. The Bible says, "When I was in prison, you visited Me." I don't compare what is in jail today to then but I do believe, strongly, being thankful has a meaning to even those who do wrong and have to spend time in jail. If you wish to help in my efforts to have this dinner Thanksgiving, God bless you for any charity.

Christmas is not far away and my friends are redoing old and some worn dolls to look like new. We have about 40 dolls but of course about 200 are needed. I have been saving toys all year but the pile looks small compared to the number of kids there will be. I walk by faith and usually there is something for each child, may not be new but so little cheers children who have very little.

Yesterday a grandmother came to the Armory where I was sorting clothes and before I knew what was happening, she grabbed me and started hugging and crying. She had just come from the Judge's chambers with her son and her husband. Their son's son was awarded to him. This has been a long fight that started about 9 months ago. After broken bones, black eyes, injured ears, some deep cigarette burns and the latest, a car lighter burn deep in his leg that is still not healed after months of treatment. This little three year old (now) is out of danger. The mother and boy friend will not be prosecuted. That seems unfair. Two more cases are pending on other children. Two children's cases are being ignored. Born to cry! I see it, feel it, live it and fight it!

I am still filling out tons of papers and trying to get disability for those who justly deserve it, it is harder by the day. I am still trying to fight the unjust labor laws and Worker's Comp cases that are often so unfair.

I need Lanoxin .125, B-D Lo Dose Syringe, Humulin N 100U/ML. Lozol 2.5 Tab, Alprazolam, Zantac 150, for different folks.

I need a gas range for a little single mother of a four year old. It cannot be over thirty inches wide. The girl is working five days a week and going to college two days and three nights a week. After her husband left her she has lived several places but lately living with her family. I heard about a little house, just for taking up the payment she could have for her own. The payments were 1/2 what her rent was. She needed closing cost. I managed this for her, got her an ice box for two hundred (with donations from those who believe in my causes). She needs a table and chairs for the kitchen. We have two sheets, two blankets and are working on things for the kitchen. The son is in Head Start, and he is learning fast. I think we have made a wonderful start.

Everything you have done for me, even if just a thought, prayer or few dollars, I thank you. The papers do not run much about my work (my causes never stop). This makes for few donations, but you still know I am out here and realize I can't make a difference in anyone's life without help.

My daughter, Joannie, and grandson, Daniel, are still here with us. She is a great help answering the phone, taking messages and giving advice about doctors, medications and problems. She is a registered nurse. She is in heart failure from cancer treatment on her heart but her determination is tremendous. She has been sorting clothes at the Armory with me all this week, getting the clothes give-away ready. Folks drop off things on my porch daily. I think there is over 100,000 pounds of clothing at the Armory, (well, maybe not quite). We have about two hundred coats. A warm coat is something you probably take for granted. You just slip into it without ever thinking what you would do if you had none, but many face this question every winter.

I went into a house with my sister late one night a few winters ago to see about a sick baby. There was no fire wood or warmth what so ever. There was no furniture, and the four children were laying on a pile of rags, and an old hound dog was laying beside them and all were huddled and shaking. The daddy had walked to a phone to call me. My sister could not stand it (in fact has not gone any where with me, to see about anyone, since). She said when we got into the car, "I'd rather be dead – I could not stand living like that." I said, "Some folks do not know life as you do. Others have known so little in life until they never expect comfort, warmth, love, a "filled feeling." They do not know security or conveniences only pain, cold, heat, dirt. I went to see an older lady and noticed her swelled leg and ankle. I told her "what are you taking for your swelling legs?" It looked terrible to me. She looked at me rather puzzled and said, "Leg swelling?"

November 6, 1994

We had the clothes give-away, and I still have not mailed this letter. This has laid on my desk over a week. The give-away was a big success! Many came and took and were so thankful. Many wanted blankets and bedspreads. There just was not enough to go around. I watched little children try on shoes, some tried shoes on another child, probably a bother or sister. Each child was so patient. Mothers walked and brought several children and left with several large plastic trash bags. Mothers struggle, and the children help. We plan another give-away in mid-January, 1995.

November 16, 1994

I have been working on many projects but the biggest one of course is the Thanksgiving Dinner. We hope to feed about 1,000. My antique customers have been bringing canned goods and some gave donations for this big dinner. It is far from ready, but the supplies are trickling in, and I am trickling out. I will start cooking hens and de-boning (100). I have had some wonderful volunteer help from my church. We also have had 6 bushels of sweet potatoes donated. I will have help from my wonderful church. They promised to gather at the church on Monday before Thanksgiving and undertake this chore.

A beautiful blonde Lab showed up at my house. He is skinny

now. I plan to fatten him. Do you need a (9 month old) male Lab that is the smartest, playingest, friendly and loving dog I have ever seen? I have picked up strays or lost dogs for many years, but this dog loves children and people and is great! I would love to keep him but my grandson, who lives with us, has asthma and is allergic to dogs. He is yours for a good home and a square meal every day. He is growing and robust, strong and full of energy. He had rather play than eat!

November 22

We have been gathering donated food, running like crazy. I will be cooking at the Patterson Cafeteria again this year. This is a wonderful place, lots of space and modern equipment. It is a far cry from the many years I cooked under primitive circumstances. There have been about 40 people say they would show up between 4:30 a.m. and noon to help with the chores and deliveries. I had thought I would have to do without bread and milk but ordered it today and "charged it." The company said I could pay after the dinner. I ordered chocolate milk for the children, 400 half pints and 200 white milk and 14 gallons for the potatoes.

November 25, 1994

The Thanksgiving Dinner was a big success! We fed 914. We fed the elderly, disabled, Hospice patients, lonely, those without food, food stamps, money, a place to cook and also homeless and transients. I think what brought the house down was an elderly woman in her 80's came for two carry outs and ask to speak to the kitchen help. I took her to the kitchen. She had bright red lipstick put on sideways and her blonde hair tightly curled. She stood before a kitchen filled with busy and tired folks and said a few simple words. "I want to tell you, me and my sister had nothing to prepare and without you we would have had no Thanksgiving Dinner today." She turned with tears and her carry outs and disappeared.

The day before the dinner a lady had called who had called earlier, and she wanted to ask me a big favor. She said she would not mind if I said no. She asked could she please have two more plates delivered to her house. She and her husband are disabled, very poor and have no transportation. I told her of course! I asked (don't know why I took the time but then lots of strange things make up my life).

I said "are you having company?" She started crying and said her two daughters and their six children were coming in so instead of 2 plates they needed 4. I asked, "Four? That is not enough." She said, "Oh, the grown folks can eat something and the four plates can be divided among the children." Of course, 10 plates were sent to this humble home!

December 1, 1994

(I promise I will get this out this week.)

I am working on the Christmas toys, sorting and gathering used toys. If you have any children or grandchildren get their cast-off toys and clothes and shoes, to me quick! There is so much to do and so little time. A little must stretch so far. Remember my 400 little children and their families in your prayers and if you have used things I will be happy to use them in my work and this endeavor. You are so precious to remember me. I know this newsletter is choppy, but I lead a choppy life. I woke running one morning, got my jeans on, did the dishes after breakfast, started grabbing up dirty clothes, decided to run to the post office. I had a time getting out my front door, opening the van door, when I got to the post office I was out of breath. I was trying to manage to get the front door of the post office open and wrestling to get out my key to open my box. I never had such a time going to the post office. I looked down, trying to get my key in the keyhole of my box, and realized I had an arm full of dirty clothes! I had been carrying them around and even drove to the post office, went in with them in my arms!! I thought, "When you carry loads until you forget you have them, maybe you have carried too many loads!!

Please have a wonderful holiday. Know we love you and thank God for you. If you have things you do not use and wish to recycle them, remember my people. Bring them to me or get them to Arkadelphia to Gay, our daughter, (246-7376) or Kandy Cayce in Little Rock (835-3013). They come often and bring what folks left on their porches. I am always thankful!!!

JoAnn Cayce

May 5, 1994

Dear Faithful Friends,

I promised myself several weeks ago I was going to put aside this day to write you and tell you some of the things that are going on or have gone on with my causes here. I had no appointments to take folks to the doctor today, and I felt I could (perhaps) stay home from rounds today. Then I had an accident and was suppose to go back to the doctor to have an x-ray of my cheek bone and eye today. I decided this morning to cancel that second appointment as it looks better, and the swelling is gone down and most of the "black eye" has disappeared. I really had a bad eye and cheek. I mashed it in the car door (that's the truth). My poor would ask me when I saw them, especially the teenagers and little children, "Mrs. Cayce, who hit you?" It is sad that they think accidents cannot happen and all black eyes and faces swelled and cuts are beatings.

As you know, it has been some months since I wrote you. I have been to Washington D.C. twice. I went after we had the big feed for Thanksgiving (we fed about 950). This visit was to unveil my portrait in the Caring Institute Hall of Fame. It was very humbling, and we enjoyed it so much. The second visit was in January to represent the State of Arkansas before the Senate concerning the health needs of the poor, elderly and those who are disabled without insurance. This speech was carried on CNN and will soon be in commercials on nationwide TV. I gave my permission last week for them to use it at no charge. I tell you this only so you will know I am not making anything from this. Never have I received money for such. If I did I would use it for the good of my poor folks – would be nice.

While in Washington this last time, Ted Kennedy, Simon, Mitchel, Pryor, Bumpers and Senator Moss all met with me, and several told me they did not know some of the things I told them concerning the problems out here, especially with the poor elderly. I mentioned to them that there was a $3,000 limit on their resources, and if they even had an old pick-up truck they were over the limit and were not allowed commodities, Medicaid, HEAP assistance, electrical assistance, hardly any food stamps, Weatherization, Project Deserve, Good Neighbor funds, etc. I insisted they consider, seriously, raising this to at least $10,000. If a man and woman have lived together for 40 and more years they have accumulated some furniture, a garden spot, a means of conveyance, maybe ever a tiller, mower, barn, horse or cow – any of these things are counted. If a widow or widower is left, his or her limit of resources in only $1,800. They cannot get any help if over that amount. Most need the medicine help badly.

One of the saddest cases, medically, I am working on right now is a man with no pancreas, not much liver, no stomach, spleen, gall bladder, bowels, etc. who, because of unknown reasons (to me) had to have surgery, was in hospital for 7 months, out for two weeks and back for three months. He has worked hard all his life and never been on the system. He is 40. He has no income and no insurance and Social Security has turned him down two times. I have appealed his case, of course. He has also had nerve damage that controls his hand, his shoulder and neck. This pain is all the time. I took him to a doctor who saw him this week in El Dorado, and this doctor looked him in the face and said, "I know you need help with all your problems but since you have no money and no insurance, there is just nothing I can do for you."

Another sad case is a woman who has had 8 blood clots in her legs and no income, money or insurance. She is slightly mentally retarded. I am taking her to the University (running up a big bill) and trying to get proof of her disability. She has high blood pressure, a disabled son, and her husband left her. She is homeless and living with folks right now who cannot keep her with only food stamps for she and her 14-year-old son. She needs medication and shelter, etc. Another case is a lady who needs five kinds of medication for life threatening situations and has no money, insurance, aid of any kind and is living with a person who just took her in. They have also taken in an elderly man with no place to go. She weighs less than 90 pounds.

I have a retarded mother of two whose husband left her, and they need food, linens, towels and a couch.

I have another mother who has two children, an alcoholic abusive husband who is under peace bond not to come near her. She has been beaten so much she is mentally off. The children, a little boy 3 and a girl 5, need clothes and sandals. They need money to have the electricity turned on, a months rent and food.

I need size 12 and a pair of 13 shoes for a father and son who came here from New York to take care of his mother. She has cancer. They had to leave what they had up there. Their shoes have worn out, and they need shoes badly. They could use some large size clothes, pants and shirts too. They have got some that are badly worn but their shoes are just gone. The boy is in the 12th grade and trying to finish. They seem like very clean, nice, polite folks.

Betty from Leola is 38 years old – worked at a furniture factory 16 years, has no insurance or income. She just had her 3rd stroke. Each time she went back to work. This time she cannot speak. She needs food, medication and her electricity turned on.

Of course I get requests to help with medication almost daily. Hungry families come almost daily to see if anyone has left any food. I always can use gas money for my van. There is not a day goes by without sad cases coming to the door or calling on the phone. Seems doctors and medication are the most needed.

On a lighter note, wanted to tell you about our tea we had Christmas. I know this may be old news but we did something we have never done before. I had the Thanksgiving Dinner and it was a huge success. We had a fair, nice day and many who had no transportation walked and came. One family of 9 came and the 10-year-old ate two plates of food, but he drank 9 pints of milk. A man came from Pennsylvania to help with this dinner. He stayed with us about four days, and, since he was a florist and decorator, he asked me about putting up my Christmas tree while he was here. He did this and then said he would like to decorate my dining room and the mantle. I said, "Here is some money, get all the stuff out of the attic in the way of decorations, and have at it." He decided to do some tables, the front porch, the columns, up the stairs and one thing led to another until he had this old house looking like a Christmas Garden. After he went home, Joannie and I decided to have open house for poor children. This developed into having a formal tea for little children from middle class homes to the poorest of the poor. We worked on this three weeks at every opportune time we could. We baked, bought and begged all kinds of cookies, candy, mints, punch, coffee, tea, chocolate, sandwiches, filled crackers, etc. We ended up with teachers, sponsors, aids, and volunteers.

If you could have seen those children come in our front door. It was like standing on the wall of heaven watching bankrupt sinners getting their first glance of the streets of gold. We had the house smelling with every good smell. In fact, one mother who could not read or write got a neighbor to write for her telling us how much she thanked us for all the trouble and expense to allow her little girl to see our house and enjoy the party. The letter said "Thanks for giving my little girl the opportunity to go into the first real pretty house she had ever been in that smelled so good." I know the child had to tell the mother how good everything smelled or the mother would not have known. I wept over that letter and our daughter living here with us, did too. We had groups of 25 or 30 each come about an hour and 15 minutes apart. They stayed an hour and we had 15 minutes to get ready for the next group. This went on from 10:00 in the morning 'til 2:30. I enjoyed doing Christmas, as always, for about 400 children but this tea, with all the fancy frills and seeing the children gaze up the stairs, seeing all the draped greenery, flowers and bells, silver and gold angels, candles lit everywhere, and Joannie even fixed a Santa on skis going over snow mountains in front of a high tree in the den. They would have sat for hours watching this. It was electric, and as Santa would get up on top of the mountains and start down they would all scream. The VCR camera captured one little girl putting candy and cookies, off plates children had left, into her pockets during the first group so seeing this we decided hurriedly to give out bags. So with several bushels of apples, oranges, candies, we filled Ziploc bags for each child as they left to take to those at home. (This was a wonderful idea.)

We are now getting ready to have a spring party. We would also like to have a trip for children this summer. These things take money, and it is a source of worry deciding if the money I have (it is so limited) should be used for things like this or medicine and doctors if I have to make a choice. I think if we can touch a child's life with something better than he has, even for a day, it will be something they can draw on in days to come. Rats, cockroaches, filth, flies, and sleeping on the floor or rags is often the only thing many have. Some know nothing but drugged or drunk and violent parents, with kicking and licks along the way.

We took a mother and her children to Little Rock, and this was a sight. To watch them grab their breath in the elevator, get big eyed at the escalator, select food from Luby's Cafeteria rows and rows of goodies was something there is nothing like. They all enjoyed the mall and seeing the people, but one thing they will never forget is the tall buildings, zoo, and just walking around in a big store. They did not have to buy anything, didn't expect anything, just to see it was all they expected.

I just wanted to write you today and let you know I am still out here. *Arkansas Democrat-Gazette* will not print things or letters about my causes like the *Gazette* used to, not that I want the publicity but would love to have some mention because it gets a little money or attention for my people and sometimes is a means of help for certain problems. If you ever have things you wish to give away or if God touches you to help in anyway, I promise you I will surely see that the most needy receive relief. I lost my warehouse and bought the house next door to me to store things so your furniture give-aways, household items as well as clothes, food, medicine you can't take or some deceased person left, will be used. I have a druggist who uses this for my folks in such a way that helps many. I can use insulin if it is in date. I send the diabetics to him. In this way folks are helped so much. It is terrible to have diabetes but it is far more sad to die for want of needles and insulin. It is hard to see terrible infections, infected ears, and abscessed teeth and not be able to do something. Donations are greatly appreciated and used (every dime) to help someone. I never ask for them and am not now, but must tell you that is something I pray for daily.

Sincerely,
JoAnn Cayce

Dear Precious Friend, Thank you!!

I acknowledge receipt of your contribution to my charity account. I am so thankful. Please know there are many needs and you have helped so much.

You probably don't realize how much you encourage me and help me to keep on going. There are so many organizations and charities, and I believe most of them are large and worthy, but none could appreciate it or need help more. I weep at the needs. I am so small and have so little and have to stretch so far. I do not know how you continue to have faith in me but I believe with all my heart God pointed your charity toward me. I have captured so many of His promises if I will but have faith and continue to pray the needs will be met.

Here are a few of the needs just this week. I am going to do my best for each one but there are so many needs.

Yesterday Ralph called from a pay phone. He is out of insulin, needles, heart medication, blood thinner, and his arthritis medication is gone. He still has not received his disability from Social Security. I have appealed and also appeared before the Federal Law Judge. He has about given up. He just got out of the hospital, with another heart blockage, and there is nothing coming in to pay the bill, the utilities are off, and the rent is three months overdue. His wife has one hand, and it is deformed badly. She has no way to work. Your money will help Ralph.

Also yesterday Billy ----- age 44 needs five prescriptions, food and shoes for her child. Her husband left because of her health problems, and he could not help her. He was overwhelmed and depressed. I try to understand that, and I'm trying to teach her to lay bitterness down. I had no money to help her except with some rice and a few canned goods.

Betty Jo ----- is 42. She lives in a shack with her unemployed daughter and 18-month-old grandchild. She has worked in a furniture factory for 13 years. She has had three massive strokes and now is unable to use one side. Each time she had a stroke she went right back to work. She has no insurance. This last stroke left her totally unable to work and about this time her daughter was laid off at a fish hatchery. She needs so much medication and also needs to go into the hospital and let them determine the cause of these strokes. She is nearly six foot tall and about 90 pounds.

Then today we made an appointment for Sara -----. Her teeth are hurting so badly. They are rotted off even with the gums. I am putting all these things to you bluntly, but I want you to understand whom you are helping, and that this is not a huge organization – it is a one on one, face to face, relief program that I have done for over 44 years. I feel you should know these are real people, with real problems, with no hope or help. When a father goes to prison and leaves a wife and little children, it is about three months before she can get food stamps or Medicaid cards for the little ones. I am the only program out here to reach or catch those who fall through the cracks. ABC newsmen came and spent time with me a few years ago. How they heard about me or why they came I do not know. Nothing ever came of it that I know of. Certainly no money ever got to me for my people, but the men were so nice, and I went about my rounds as usual. I went to see about twins who were born at home and weighted about 2 pounds each. They had no bed, clothes and their mother was 14-years-old and living in an abandoned house. The men could not bring their cameras and equipment up on the porch all at one time or the old porch would fall in. (It fell in about three weeks later and literally the entire house became totally unlivable.) But I had the tiny scrap of humanity in my hands trying to listen to the rattle in its chest, and one of the cameramen got really close over my shoulder, and I glanced back, and as I did he was wiping a tear rolling down his cheek. I later asked him if they did not have poverty and things like this in New York. He said they did but then he said, "Mrs. Cayce where I live there is help just around the corner – many organizations and programs. But I have seen today, going around with you and seeing this rural area, there is no help for these folks but you if the system is not working for them." This is so very true.

Those the system leaves out have no place to go. Until the system kicks in, folks can get mighty hungry. I have spent a lifetime begging for people. Some of these are the third generation. My mother did this before me, and I have heard her cry over the death of someone that a few dollars would have saved, but she had no donations or help.

Thank you with all my heart for your help. I know you are unselfish folks. I don't understand how folks have money to give away, but I am so thankful, even through I have no money to give, I have a life of service I can give. God knows I give willingly.

A young boy with multiple problems went to prison last month because he had no money to buy his medication, his mother's medication or get them a place to live. I was working as hard as I could on his and her disability so they could have SSI from Social Security. It was not fast enough. He was delivering some crack for $100 and got busted. He is in the hospital in bed all the time in prison. The system could have saved lots of money had they helped him. He has no pancreas and has to swallow pills every five minutes while he eats and take 4 insulin shots of two different kinds with CLEAN needles (lots of my poor use the same needles over and over because I cannot buy new packages ($11 for 100 needles). He took many kinds of medication, and they took his Medicaid card and his mother's because he turned 18, and at this age, mothers and children are cut off. I know he did not do the right thing pushing that dope, but he did what he thought was the only thing to do. He told me he had been in three comas in more than a week because he had no insulin. Children's Hospital took him until he was 18, but they do not see to someone after age 18.

Again, I am so happy about your donation. I will be so careful with it. I hope to have some when school starts so I can have some school supplies. I wish I knew a company that makes pencils and tablets who would let me have their culls. I have never written any companies and ask for anything except rice.

I hope you will understand when I tell you, I love you.

Sincerely,

JoAnn Cayce

June 8, 1995

Dear Sweet and Faithful Friends:

This charity letter is long overdue. Thanks to each of you who have continued to love and support all my causes. Thanks, certainly, to those of you who have prayed for them and me. It is hard to make it out here, sometimes seems like a jungle. But, when I think I have a time getting around to all my causes and people, I think about the problems the people have, and I am ashamed to complain when all I need is energy and a few dollars to keep a purpose afloat.

This morning I have been working with a man who has lost his SSI. I will have much paper work to fill out and will try to keep him in groceries and medicine until I can get the system to kick in (if it ever does). This man had been on SSI for about six years after he got hurt and never, never has been "right" since. He failed to fill out his report. Can't read or write and just put mail in the trash, so they stopped his checks. For eight months he has had no high blood pressure medication, insulin, nothing much to eat and has been living in an old trailer. He put sides and a roof on it out of scraps and calls it home. I went to a local doctor this morning and told them he needed his blood sugar and blood pressure taken. They did this free. I will get the reports in the morning. I ask him if he knew he could die not taking his insulin and blood pressure medication. He said he knew this. In fact, he said "that passed through me." He is retarded and has no transportation. Many problems in rural areas are due to no transportation.

This case is like so many – they do not know which way to turn. Sometimes they go to the welfare office, and so much proof is required, and they are so illiterate and discouraged they simply give up. Often mothers of small children will let the family go hungry because they simply are too unequipped, mentally, to manage. This is one way I spend so much time – managing cases. I think there should be a building, somewhere, filled with case workers who are kind, sweet, sympathetic and anxious to walk someone through the system then be willing to supplement the needs when the system has no way or while it is "kicking in." It is so hard (and expensive) to keep a family alive while they wait.

I was invited to Washington two weeks ago to speak on behalf of the elderly and tell their troubles and problems to the Senate and the Investigating Committee. I absolutely could not go. Several cases were coming up in court that I had to represent in Social Security cases. I think it is a shame the ones who write the rules do not even know the need of those they write the rules for. The resource limit of the elderly is too low. If they have an old pick-up truck, old worn out lawn mower, an old cow or few chickens and a run down shack, and it appraises for more than $3,000, they are disqualified for everything. This excludes them from medication, doctors, commodities, HEAP, and all assistance for any free utilities. It they are alone the resource limit drops to $1,600 for one elderly person. To me it should be at least $10,000 for two.

I went out to an old man's shack a few weeks ago, and his feet were mostly on the ground. I had just had a clothes give-away and gave away everything that had been donated. I asked his shoe size and said, "You really need some shoes." He was old, worn out, thin and hopeless. He said, "Well Ms. JoAnn, I can't have groceries, medicine and shoes too." Thank goodness for a gift in the mail that allowed me to take him some good soft tennis shoes.

School is out and children are home (such as some have), and I worry so about their food. They were fed at school and this was all some got to eat. I will spend lots of time this summer checking cupboards to see what there is to eat, inside. I am getting very low on groceries to give out. I have a couple boxes of canned goods but no meat, bread, dried milk, eggs, oleo, sugar, flour, meal or chickens. Some have garden things planted and this will help some. I need money for cereal and fruit. Children cut their feet and step on nails in summer and have little attention. I watch for this. Some children are so starved for folic acid that they will eat lemons and limes and oranges, rind and all! I don't say anything when they grab them and start chewing on the rind. I wish I had a truck load of fruit to give out weekly.

Battered women and scared little children are almost a weekly occurrence. So many have no place to go and nothing to go in. I need Ensure or food supplement for the sick, malnourished and those who have serious physical problems. Of course I need gas money to take folks to doctors and clinics, and just to ride up and down the road, house to house. I have women who have no Medicaid cards who need mammograms. They are high risk because a mother, sisters or both have died from breast cancer. It is very hard to get a Medicaid card these days. I have never asked for money, but some of you send any way, and it sure comes in handy. Not a penny is wasted.

I need used bikes for folks to have transportation. Of course kids love bikes, but some use bikes for all the shopping, doctors, etc. One lady I got a bike for last year picks up cans riding her bike. This enables her to have lights. She pays her light bill with money from discarded cans.

Someone gave me a good used couch the other day, and I took it to a lady in a very bad area who takes in children off the streets while parents are working or off somewhere. They were having to sit on the floor. She had a room and an old used TV someone gave her but no chairs. She shouted and thanked God for a faded used couch I delivered to her. I thought as I drove home how I had been complaining to myself that I had to go home and fix supper and I had a cabinet full to choose from. Here was a lady who wished she had enough to feed the children, sitting in her spare room, their supper. This business will really keep you humble.

I learned a lesson on motherhood yesterday just at the right time. I had a mother who was so "no good." Her children suffer greatly. They are born to cry. I had begun to wonder if there were any "good" mothers among my rounds yesterday. Going home, I went by our house to get the food to feed the strays I feed each day. I went down to the place where I honk my horn and feed a little dog I have been feeding over a year. She has been so badly treated I have never been able to touch or put my hands on her. She will dance around me and wag her tail, but, like so many little children I see, she wants loving badly but is terrified of people. She had puppies a month ago. I knew the puppies would be following her out of the bushes in a few days for something to eat. I planned to put some food inside a bread wrapper and lay it by the mother's food so she could "wag a bag" to them. I thought, "Well they may not be old enough to eat yet." I decided to use my oldest test. I had a chicken leg left on a saucer in our ice box so I put it right in the top of the mother's feed. When I honked she came out of hiding. She grabbed that chicken leg, but, hungry as she was, she laid it carefully aside and she ate the old dry dog-food. Then she carefully took that chicken leg in her mouth and carried it "home" to her babies. I had to have a little cry wishing some others I knew would be willing to do without (crack, alcohol, cigarettes) so their babies could have milk, cereal and eggs.

Many want to know "how this business works" and what I do. There is never a dull moment. Yesterday I had a full day. An alcoholic came, down in his back, could hardly walk, begging for help. He was in such need, hungry, in pain and could not straighten up. He needed everything including a friend. The doctor wrote me a letter asking me to help the man. Times like this when I am in such a hurry, the day is already planned, I need to be three places at once, I have to stop and think about Jesus. He told us about a man, who fell among thieves. Many passed him by, as he lay beside the road. Finally a Good Samaritan came by. There was the example I should follow. So now I have taken on another case needing food, medicine, a job and a "drying out."

Yesterday I went to see a woman who has cancer. She was bald from treatment. She had sent for me. She needed medication, someone to write a letter to her doctor. She reminded me before I left how she used to visit my mother and how mother was always so kind. From her house I went to a fellow who had fixed up an old dilapidated trailer. To him it is a paradise. All I could see was a pile of scrap medal with spiders climbing on it. But I gave him a used couch (that did not want to go through the door) and you would have thought I had given him Rockefeller's best race horse. In fact, I don't think Rockefeller ever had a race horse he was more proud of than this man was of his humble home. But then, I doubt, Rockefeller has never spent one night in the cold, with only the groans of an empty stomach to keep him awake.

At another house a mother had called for help. Her 12-year-old had eye trouble. Turned out he had 20/40 in one eye and 20/20 in the other eye. Family had no transportation, insurance, or money for help, and the child needed a specialist. Another of my calls from a young retarded boy, who had saved enough money to buy a lawn mower at Wal-Mart, wanted me to meet him there and pick it out and then take him and the mower back to the country. He planned to walk. I told him I could come by and get him. Now he is the proud owner of a lawn mower, and believe me, it looks better than the house he lives in with his grandmother. Last night I took another retarded adult back to Wal-Mart at closing time to shop. He cannot count money or read prices. It was a long day!

A few weeks ago the Sheriff called and said they had an old man who had not been embalmed in the cooler waiting for money to bury him. Said he died in the nursing home with no people, burial insurance, plot, suit, tie, shirt, preacher or flowers. The Sheriff said, "I have heard you bury folks in this condition." I had just okayed the dentist (to the tune of $200) to pull a poor lady's teeth that day, and of course, I could not call this off. So being short I got on the phone. Volunteers dug the grave, a family donated the plot, the florist offered flowers, my sister-in-law and 2 checks that came in the mail, and I split the cost of the bargain casket. I prayed for a suit all day. We had had a clothes give-away, and no suits were left. Late that afternoon, a lady came by with bags of clothes in her back seat. I just knew a nice suit was in those bags. She started telling me her husband died two years before and she had not been able to part with his clothes. I finally butted in and said, "Do you have a suit, white shirt, and tie in these bags?" She said, "No, my husband has some nice suits and shirts, but I just can't part with them yet." I said, "Could I follow you home and get a suit, shirt and tie? I need to take these to the funeral home tonight." She seemed shocked at first, and I secretly vowed to some day visit and listen to her story, but right then I needed a suit or bury the man in a closed casket. After I followed her the six miles to her house, she allowed me to go through her husband's nice suits, shirts and ties and pick out an outfit. I started out her door and she hugged me and said, "I never would have thought it would feel good to give his things away."

Every day is a new challenge. There is pain, joy, frustration, laughter, prayers (lots of this), aborted plans, times when I can't believe a doctor or the system has done this to a human. Times when

I could kick a mother; like the one who saw but did nothing about her 12-year-old daughter and a 17-year-old boy sneaking around. Then she called me after the fox got in the hen house asking me to handle everything. Said a baby was "on the way." I could almost walk but I looked into the doe eyes of that child, and I will do what I can!

We just had a wonderful clothes give-away. Over 100,000 pounds were given away. We are well on our way to another big one. My porch this weekend was completely filled, but today someone dumped a half ton of garbage on the porch. Things no one could wear – dirt, bugs and rags. So, once again, in this business you've got to take the bitter with the sweet.

I still have not gotten off my income tax ... I still have not started my book ... I still have not done my spring house cleaning or taken those few days off to be with my husband that I promised. We still have not taken the grandchildren to Disney World or fishing. In fact, I could have started my Social Security a year and half ago at 62 but I just have not gone down and applied. I have taken three new cases this week but can't get my own filed. But would you believe I do just what I want to do and have no complaints. I get a little stiff and sore after lifting 100,000 pounds sorting for a clothes give-away. I pick up a cold, virus, bugs or a chill from some households, but it has been a long time since I got a real good case of head lice and even longer since the itch struck. My children don't bug me so much anymore to slow down or tell me all the bad things that are going to happen to me "at my age." My husband is reconciled to a can of tuna and chips for lunch, and he stopped long ago asking me what time I'd be home. What more can I expect at my age? Life is great and, believe you me, I think I have seen enough lives that aren't to judge!

Thank you for every thought, ever check, every bag of used items or clothes, your old shoes, blankets, toys and if any of you need a tax credit, remember my causes! There is always one and most times when you remember me with a donation is when I am asking the Good Lord to pinch someone and whisper my name in their ear!

I love you all.

JoAnn Cayce

December 13, 1995

Dear Caring Friends,

I have not gotten out a charity newsletter in months and months. Some of you may think I have retired. The newspapers ran some articles that sounded like it. They just said I was ill and did not get to have the Thanksgiving Dinner this year and told about my work.

One reporter from Pine Bluff came down and spent the entire day going around with me. She left in tears, promising to tell the poor's side. I told her I would be happy if the article turned the hearts and minds of the "Newts and Bobs" out there to understand the plight of folks who are willing to work but live in rural areas and small towns where those with educations and cars for transportation can't find work much less those who have neither.

I don't know where to start. Each day is so filled with running and calls and request and stories. I have never heard the same one twice. All cases are different and require research, prayers and leg work to see if there is an answer.

Today a family formerly from Michigan called. Believe it or not, I had seen this family walking on the road in Fordyce, and the thought struck me – that is a family in trouble or the kids would be in school. I did not have time to stop. I had gone to the Armory to sort and fix on Christmas for over 400 children and had to leave so I could pick up medicine for a very sick child. I was in a hurry when I saw this family walking. The mother had a broken arm and the man was crippled and the three children looked very cold.

When I got home, my daughter told me this family had called. They were moving to this area, wrecked the UHaul just outside of town and completely destroyed their household goods. The family was bummed up and the lady had broken her arm and dislocated her ankle. They had no food, money, place to stay, furniture, and today Human Services told them to contact me. Is that a cop out? Here I am barely able to reach the needs of families for Christmas. I have promised food, Christmas for the three boys and will try to get medical help and a place to stay. Looks like a days work, and I don't have a day (or a dollar, ha). They have no people, friends or work here. They moved (on a whim I think) to the South. They could not have landed in a poorer area. I told my daughter, I may be better off to buy five tickets back to Michigan.

Then with the cold that moved in there was a mother with only a wood stove in one room, camped out on the floor with two small children, no lights or food and a stray dog under her porch had 8 puppies. Again, the dog could not have gone to a poorer area. Blankets, food, dog food, medicine for the sick children and wood (there was so little wood left she said she was panicked to know when she burned the last stick what she would do). Her husband is in jail for battery, threatening to kill four teachers and kidnapping one of his children and his wife. (There was a peace bond against him for coming on the property.) He went to the school with a knife trying to get his second grader. The teachers stood their ground and told him he would have to kill them to get to the child. They are considered heroes.

I have Grandy's teeth pulled, and when her mouth heals, I need a set of good strong teeth. She is a 44-year-old whose teeth were so rotted she could not eat. She had called me to see if I had any Ensure. I took her some, expecting her to have cancer or some terminal disease. She had such a sore mouth she was starving because she could not eat. She is slightly retarded living with her parents, one of whom died the week before and the other in the hospital with kidney failure. The dentist said he would pull them for $197. I asked if he would charge it, and he said yes. I feel this dear soul deserves these paining teeth out. She said for over 5 years her mouth has been in constant pain, and for a year she has not been able to eat anything but liquid. She smiled so big when I told her I would help her and with run over shoes and a ragged thin dress, standing in a cold yard, said "that makes me so happy." I thought, going home, what would I do if I lived in a shack, hurt so bad I could not shut my mouth and was freezing cold with a dead father at the funeral home and no way to bury him (she told me that story) and a dying mother in the hospital. You know trouble runs so deep in many cases. Answers come very slow. I thought I had trouble a few months ago trying to bury a man who had no suit, or a burying plot, but he did have a casket. If you want to be "looked at," be a white woman in dirty blue jeans going into a black funeral home with a used suit for a nude corpse whose name you don't even know. But that is just one of the memorable moments.

I have stayed on the road lots lately trying to take folks to Little Rock to doctors. One of these is Tom. He lives in a tiny well-house that is on a vacant lot. He has no utilities, bath or windows. He burned up this summer and this winter he is freezing to death. He came through here about three years ago and got work bailing and picking up hay from a field so he "stayed." He hurt his back several months ago and called me. He cannot do any odd jobs now that requires lifting. Of course he is uneducated and there's nothing else he can do except hard manual work. I have been taking him back and forth to Little Rock. My family thinks I am crazy, not knowing the man and taking such chances, but I know all I need to know. He is a hurting person with no one to help him. He said he left home when he was 15 and doesn't know where his family is. We have to take his blood pressure every day because the doctors (first ones he has gone to in over 25 years) found he had very high blood pressure, serious kidney problems and a bad stomach, numb legs and terrible eye sight. If you want to get your heart torn out take someone like Tom to a big cafeteria and tell them you are paying and to eat all they want. Tom was different. He gets to eat only one meal a day (most times he says). He got mashed potatoes with lots of gravy, lots of bread, and I insisted he get some meat. He said, "how much is that?" Someone asked me one day who I would love to take to dinner if I could. I think they thought I would say a famous person. I honestly would take several very poor people who had never eaten out before. There is absolutely nothing like it. The joy this gives you is almost like being on a "high." They are so excited they tremble. The same goes for little children who have never been to a mall or seen the decorations at Christmas. I always dreamed of getting a group of very poor children and going to the Osborne's lighted house at Christmas and just let them stand at the fence and stare. Another big joy at this time of year is to take a tree and decorations to a family who has no tree. Of course I leave and don't try to help them decorate it. I have told our kids when they were small and we did this and they wanted to "help" the family, "This is something no one has the right to do uninvited. Let them enjoy doing it the way they want."

I want each one reading this newsletter, who has done the least thing for me to help keep my ship afloat, to know I love you and appreciate you so much. If you have not mailed me a check, that is fine I still love you and feel you have thought about what is going on out here. It is not earth shattering, but it makes up my days (in fact has made up my life), and it gives me such pleasure and peace that if I can't scrape up money for a given problem I don't feel it is a failure. I sometimes must let them know I am trying and I care. In this world we need more care. This time of year when there is so much giving floating around and I see folks throwing money away for things that are not useful or life sustaining, I feel a big catch in my throat. I think how much the giver could receive just helping a hungry family or a cold child have a coat or shoes that fit. I need good used coats for children so badly right now, I guess this is what made me say that. There were no food drives for me this December and the school did not collect toys as they always have, but we are still working on a wonderful Christmas for over 400 little children. Christmas Eve we hope there will not be a family in this area who doesn't have something. I got calls this year from as far away as 25 miles, and then stupid me went by the Human Services this week and picked up all the families who had not been adopted. Just listen to this paragraph . . . "Please help my four brothers and sisters. Our papa done lost his job cause he hurt his souther (shoulder). We all need a coat, my two brothers needs shoes and my mama needs everything. Our gas is cut off now and we out food. Help papa get job." I am happy to report I was buying Christmas candy and fruit for poor children at the wholesale house today, and I just mentioned knowing a good man who needed a job badly. They called me tonight for his name and location and said they were contacting him for work. This won't give them any Christmas money, but I believe for "papa" to find a job will give them a joyful Christmas.

I hope each of you reading this newsletter has a wonderful Christmas. I hope you and your loved ones are all together and the sweet joy of love will surround you so warmly it will be impossible for you to lose you tempers or fuss because the kitchen sink is filled with dishes. We are sure going to put our feet up (till the phone rings, ha) and just say "I am glad you are all here ... feel free to cook and clean anything." No, I am kidding we are having a big family gathering and lots of food, and I hope I can forget Ivy who lives alone in a shack and is begging for a turkey or Mrs. ----- who lives with her retarded son and is begging me to find someone who will help her "buy her and her son a ham." Merry Christmas!

Again thanks and much love.

JoAnn Cayce

October 16, 1997

Dear Friend,

It is hard to believe I have not gotten out a Charity Letter since April 30th. I am sorry about that. Things move so fast around here and there are so many things going on that absolutely can't be put off that the things I would do, often, are like choosing between suffering people and my pleasure.

I have just come from two houses and will just start with this and go backward to the happenings. I was called by a nurse and told I needed to go back in the woods and check on a family who was in great need. She said it would be hard to find them. When I ask her to describe, she said, "For example a family had picked up one of the children about 6 to get shoes for it so it could go to school. She said there were two babies, one 2-weeks-old and one 2-months." I said, "Sounds like I should take some birth control with me." She said "Yes, they need a Social or Health Dept. aid badly, but I have not been able to get one to go see about them. Someone said to call you."

It was raining this morning and had been all night. My truck had to go to the garage. It was not a time I should wander in the wet woods in my van, maybe getting stuck. I had to take someone with me who would drive me home from the garage. I packed the van with baby clothes, blankets, children's clothes, shoes, and all kinds of used things. We had to be pretty good detectives to find the place. Going to it I saw and stopped at one place that honestly was so bad I wanted to just stay. The three-year-old, at this house had swallowed thirty seizure pills. The house was a wreck even if it had been clean. There were all kinds of problems and more arriving as I was leaving, but she had told me how to get to the other house. I wanted to say "down across those woods?" when she showed me where to go in at. She said "Yes, and there are 16 of them in a four room trailer."

When we got there everything was clean, but I was met with several dogs. I started talking to them in baby language, and soon they were crawling with friendliness. All at once the porch was alive with beautiful children. The 16-year-old came out with a baby in her arms, and the mother also had a new baby. The aunt had been taken in with her five plus a baby. The husband of one woman was working but no way he could support so many. I recognized some of them and knew they had all been to my food give-away the week before. I asked, and no one answered but one beautiful little girl about 5 (so tiny) said, "Yes, we went and got food." I guess the older ones were afraid to answer, afraid they might get shut out of something I had in the van if they had been given to previously. I and the person with me started unloading boxes and bags and the squeals and laughs were heard all over the hollow. (I again thought, why is not everyone out here with a box of something trying to get my job?) The little faces were alive with pure joy. The beautiful eyes and smiles were so pretty. Even the 16-year-old who had just had a baby seemed happy someone found them. They would love to have a room built on but the only man is working so hard and so late he can't get to it. He had some lumber lying on the ground. Seems he had taken in more than he can feed or house. Lots of work to be done in the extended family – great need for volunteers (who can drive a straight nail). No doubt there will be other trips through the woods to this house – little Red Riding Hood has nothing on me, but will have to watch for the bad wolf (the black dog that sneaks up behind).

Wanted to tell you the big food give-away was two weeks ago. We spent almost everything in the charity account and now are wondering if that was wise. Now there are needs I can't reach, like a grandmother who needs her water turned on. Her little grandson was beaten by his step-father and dropped off at her house. The child had no clothes, shoes and the grandmother had no food, and the water was shut off for non-payment of the bill. It will take $90 to get it back on. I got the child some clothes from my grandson and bought him some shoes. The school called and asked me to go see about the child. (Getting the water on is just one thing that I feel so badly about not being able to do). I saw the little first grader's dirty ears when I was trying on his new shoes and thought how badly he needs a bath. Well dirty ears never killed a child, I don't guess.

Now about the food give-away. We went to the Rice Depot in Little Rock, and Laura let me have lots of good things including wieners, fried chicken (frozen) and fresh squash and chicken pot pies. We got rice, green beans, Cokes, cookies (they give away what is donated to them so don't think Cokes and cookies are things they wasted money on). The children at the give-away went wild — just wish I had some more for that bunch of children just this morning, and that little first grader at his grandmother's.

After we got all the Little Rock food to the National Guard Armory, next we went to Warren to the Bradley County Food Bank. We can buy over there for 14¢ a pound surplus and donated things from Second Harvest. We took the money we had except a tiny bit of emergency money (it is gone now) and got two small trucks, a van and a big truck full on two different trips. We took all these loads to the National Guard Armory. They had loaded the big truck with huge boxes of washing powder, Tampax, disposal diapers, baby food, canned food, cereal, etc. with a fork lift. Some of these boxes might have weighed as much as 1000 pounds. Joannie said later she was worried about how we would get it all off, but I knew if God blessed us to have money for food and get it on the truck, I would be blessed to get it off.

Before we got back to the Armory, I began to have second thoughts. I was driving the big truck and thinking "I have spent all the money now and am without money to hire labor to help us. I began to shake. I gave JoAnn a good talking to and she said, "Stop this!" It will work out – this was the food we have needed so badly. This was food needed to help keep people who had just gotten jobs going till first pay check. It was food needed for the 3,000 checks that were stopped the last six weeks. This was a wonderful time but I kept asking myself what if a child has to have an antibiotic or gets an abscessed tooth, or falls on the slide, or gets hit by a car, or gets abused, or a woman gets battered and needs stitches. I decided to not hire any help except the one young man who went with us after the food. I thought if I got asthma (it is fall) or my sugar jumped or the roof fell in, I would take it one thing at a time. I was going to keep the faith.

When we got back to the Armory I jumped off the big truck and started looking for a fork lift. The county did not have one, the city did not have one but a lumber yard right across the street from the Armory had one, and, not only did he come over with the fork lift he brought two of his hired hands in the lumber yard, and, after the fork lift got what it could off the truck, his men helped my one man and they had it off the truck in less than an hour...sitting on the Armory floor. You couldn't have touched me with a ten foot pole. I knew God was on this job and all would be well. And didn't cost me a dime.

In each family's box, we put about 20 items. We also gave out Tampax, diapers, washing power, Cokes, cookies, and three boxes of cereal to each family. Can you imagine when I had been trying to find one box of cereal in our food pantry for only families with children not on WIC? The day of the give-away, it was like waiting for a birthing (I have waited for lots of these). I called the football coach and asked for the football team to volunteer to help at the give-away. I thought with those in wheel chairs, crippled elderly, mothers with babies in arms and those on crutches they would be a wonderful help. They decided to come, and the coach wanted to come too. I thought (looking up) "You all need to see this. You will see things that will help you be strong and win games. You will see how much you have to be thankful for." Before we hardly opened the Armory doors people were overrunning us. Hundreds came. The coach ran over to me and said, "Mrs. Cayce, you don't need a football team, you need a riot squad." They were so desperate for food, diapers, washing powder, and they were so afraid they would not get any. They were so appreciative and the football boys said the elderly especially told them over and over how what they got was needed. Thank each one of you who sent a check in the last several months. Some of it went to help buy food for this give-away. We would love to have a give-away every month.

There has been so many other things, things that I thought would either thrill me to death or worry me to death. Some got their GED who had worked so hard. Some got out of trade school that had been like pulling teeth, five houses burned and had to have families set up all over again. We did this with the used things people gave us to give out. I am out of sheets, blankets, pots and pans. If you have a box please let me have them. Along with helping others we helped bury two children in the last three months. We are working with a twelve-year-old who is pregnant. She is physically and mentally handicapped. She was raped by a 35-year-old who is running from the law. This is a sad choice. I finally had to back off. The mother is deciding. She is close to 8 weeks. I also missed it with a thirteen-year-old. Got her to the Health Center for birth control and she was 2 weeks pregnant. I beat myself over and over on this one. She is also retarded.

I took a toothbrush to a 5-year-old the other day along with some used items folks sent from Lonoke – food such as jelly, syrup, peanut butter and such. He was so tickled about the toothpaste and tooth brush. In discussing its use, he tried to take it and said, "Now I won't have that 'smell' in the morning." He had seen someone who had one, and he knew all about it. He was very proud of having seen a brush before. This is America...right?

There are some who need medicine and some are choosing between medicine, food and lights. I guess that is everywhere, especially with the elderly.

It will soon be Thanksgiving. I am hoping I will be able to have another food give-away on Monday before Thanksgiving. If you would like to buy 100 pounds of food, it will only cost $14 at 14¢ a pound. I saw an old man cry because we gave him a 12 cent box of salt not too long ago. He said he did not know when he had ever had salt in his house. I will put your donation toward an emergency or medicine if you had rather. We are also trying to get coats new and used. One Human Service agency has ask for help to supply kids with coats; many also depend on us for children's coats; many are out of work, disabled who have small children. A fairly sturdy coat at the Dollar Store can be bought for from $15 to $22.

I am not begging, I am just giving you the opportunity if you want to help. Some will get this letter and help every month. You can't imagine how I depend on this. I thought others might want to help. There is no administrative cost in my charity work. I have also never taken a salary off the top, but I think most all of you know that.

On the lighter side: Not long ago I had to get over 400 boxes for a clothes give-a-way and stopped by all the grocery stores and really fell short, so I stopped at the liquor stores. They always have nice sturdy boxes. I was trying to explain to someone why I was there. The doctor, told me, "Mrs. Cayce, no matter where we see you we know you are helping someone." I thought about and rejoiced in what he said, and then I ran into the new motel manager at the motel. I had gone in to ask about a motel room for a couple hours. I saw the look on his face and quickly told him I needed the room for a family of ten to take a bath. One of the maids started telling him about me. The man ended up wanting to furnish the room free. You know it is hard to remember when dealing with a new person, they shock very easily.

There are lots of good people out here. I went to Wal-Mart to get a pair of shoes this week for a very pitiful child. I had measured his little dirty foot against a size 4 tennis shoe of my grandson I had taken over to the shack. His little foot was about and inch and half shorter than a size 4. I went to Wal-Mart and told the clerk. She got the shoes and asked, "Do you think these two pairs will do?" I said, "Oh I don't want both pairs I am just trying to get the right size." I held one to the bottom of the other and I could see it was really getting hard for her to understand. I finally told her, quickly, the circumstances. Her eyes filled and when I decided which size I wanted, she pulled out a twenty dollar bill and said, "Mrs. Cayce, I am glad to meet you. I have heard about you for years. Will you let me buy this kid a pair of tennis shoes?" I knew the poor woman probably worked a day at take home pay for that amount. I hugged her and thanked her and the people passing probably thought "There's that crazy Mrs. Cayce hugging some woman in Wal-Mart, no telling what that is about."

A couple weeks ago, I heard about a lady who worked in the Deli of one of the local grocery stores. I was told she was working trying to pay for burying her child. I went straight to the store (while some were wondering what to do). I ask someone in the store where the lady was who lost a child. They pointed her out to me, and she was elbow deep in dirty dish water with a huge pan scrubbing it. I went behind the display case and told her who I was (it really didn't matter), and I said, "I'd like to put something in your apron pocket to help you with your problem." She grabbed me, dishwater and all and said "Thank you!" I didn't have to explain me to her nor did she have to bare her soul to tell me her problem. Any human being alive would know that woman would not be scrubbing pots and pans with a breaking heart if she didn't have to. Reach out friends...it doesn't have to be proper, or even explained. If it comes from your heart and relieves pain, sorrow and need, it is right and beautiful. (I should know.) I can remember the old days on a day when I was in the Super Market looking. I was trying to make 400 pounds of turkey and dressing with one turkey and almost choking, wishing I had more money. A lady, I did not even know, came up to me and said, "Mrs. Cayce, are you cooking for the elderly and poor this year?" I said, "Yes." She said, "I have just been given a turkey by my boss at work, and we don't even eat turkey, could I give it to you?" I went out and got the turkey, but I shook for hours. I remember asking God to forgive me that I had accused Him of not seeing to my needs. Of course in later years I cooked 800 pounds of dressing and had 40 turkeys, but I tried to stay humble all year long because God has a way of slapping my face to the dust by being so good to me, it is a terrible whipping.

I love each of you, and even if you do not find it in your heart to help me at this time of the year, help somebody. It is each of our privilege to give back, after all, there but for the grace of God we may need medicine, food, a coat, relief from a light, gas or water bill. Shake hands with a blessing by touching someone who needs a touch, often times from your hip pocket.

JoAnn Cayce

November 27, 1997

Dear Friends,

Today is late on Thanksgiving. I have been delivering but am back home and determined to get these thank yous off while my mind is so touched with each of you and those you helped.

Your donation of clothes or money has arrived, and I cannot express my thanks giving and deep appreciation for your love and support. I gathered all the donations of money that came in and was so proud of every cent. I counted the money and prayed hard. Most of it went for food and medicine. We went to the Rice Depot and got all the food we could in the big truck, it is free. They did not have much – only five bags of rice and last time we were able to get thirty. They have 25 (I think) pounds in each bag We try to put five pounds in each box in each of 500 baskets. We also got a few other things but they were low because so many food banks were coming for Thanksgiving. We were thankful for what we got because it was free. Praise God. Then we went (Tuesday) to Warren to the Bradley County Food Bank where I can buy for 14¢ a pound. We have a ton and half truck with a huge box on back we use for the antique shop, and I have always used my trucks in my "poor business" also. We filled it from front to back solid with food. I got about $2,000 worth this load, and we go back Monday. I came home feeling like Santa must when he leaves the North Pole with the sleigh packed. Thanks to those of you who mailed donations for Thanksgiving. I could not do without you. I am saving food also and going to buy another truck load or two if possible for the big food give-away the 13th of Dec. On this date we will give out food to nearly 1,000, and in the afternoon with the young people who are volunteering and those who come down for the weekend from Ill. Mo. and Ind., will make nearly 1,000 stockings filled with apples, oranges, candy, pencils, etc. What ever comes in or we can buy. These will be tied with huge red ribbons and will go to about 600 little needy children for Christmas and to the nursing homes, the disabled and elderly on the night of the 17th and on the 19th (children).It will take 15 bushels of apples, 15 bushels of oranges and 300 pounds of candy and ten days of work, off and on, getting it all delivered. I have to save some donations to help buy wood for families. Some get to cut wood on the halves, but some single moms who are blessed with a little job depend on me to find some wood or manage for some. My son and family sometimes help with that. They will be here the 15th.

All the time this is going on all the regular things are happening – abused kids, battered wives, sick folks, medicine needs and troubles that even I can't imagine – different ones all the time. Plus the names of needy children will get called in, also directions to homes and trying to make sense out of the calls left on the answering machine. Sometimes these would be funny if they were not so pitiful. Some will say, "Is that you Mrs. Cayce? Is it, no it ain't." etc. Some ask the answering machine to not tell anyone but me.

I do thank those of you who have mailed in clothes. Some sent boxes of gifts, toys, clothes, coats, shoes, tooth paste, brushes and many things I can use espically this time of the year. We are really going to start moving toys to the Armory and have been working on dolls. Anyone that can comb hair and hold a needle we have on the volunteer list. Some folks avoid us like the plague, ha. Every ballgame, my daughter takes a box of bathed dolls and combs, brushes, and clothes and tells anyone (that smiles at her or asks what she is doing) about the 250 used dolls who need loving care. We have about 110 finished. We also have 120 basketballs that need blowing up and washing. They were given because no one wanted to work on them. Some can be fixed, and some are past the point of no return. How I wish I could get in Mattel's toy factory and be told I could have all I could pack in 2 hours. I dream dreams like that. But God is good – He gave me you.

I have had some problems and doctor thought I was having some strokes. Since Oct. first I needed to get checked out. I went for an MRI yesterday at UAMS in Little Rock and seems all is alright, and these are my old migraines returning and causing some difficulty speaking and moving my hand and arm and swallowing. Anyway, as I was leaving yesterday I had to go to the pharmacy to get some prescriptions filled. My husband and I went up to the cash register when our name was called to pick up the medication and pay. A young woman about 35 was standing at the register. She said, "The doctor wants me to get started on it today." The pharmacist said, "Yes you need it badly, but we cannot charge it to you." The lady said, "Could I see a Social Worker?" She was told they all went home at 4, and it was 5:10. She said, "The medicine is $62, what do you want to do?" It was clear the ragged lady had no money, and I thought the poor think a miracle will fall from the sky, and I realized I had to be that miracle. I pressed two 20's in her hand and said "God has blessed me greatly I want to help you." With my money she lacked more still. She gave all she had to the lady behind the desk and said, "Could I get $46 worth?" All time she was telling me and my husband "God love you, God bless you, praise the Lord." One doctor behind came up hearing her, and said, "Let me get my Bible – we are going to have a revival." Some more in line heard her and said, "Yes, Lord." The pharmacist behind the register said, "Listen lady, I am paying the rest of your medicine He has blessed me too, and I need to show Him I am thankful. Take the medicine and go home." She was hugging folks and told my husband as she left, "Give me your address, and I will maybe be able to send you the money." My husband said, "She is known as the Arkansas Angel. She doesn't want you to pay her back."

I cannot tell you the good things that have happened lately. I met a very old couple who both needed a coat and their shoes were gone, and the old man walked so crippled. My husband went for an eye exam for his glaucoma. I was so touched by the obvious poverty of the two I had to find out more about them. I ask her where they lived, and she said, "Out in the country passed Sherwood, Arkansas." She said her husband was shot as a boy hunting squirrels when he was 16. He laid the gun down and it went off striking him too high to remove his leg. She said he has worked all his life in pain doing odd jobs, walking into town to work. She said, "Now he is going blind, and we ain't got no money." They were fine decent people I could tell. She looked like something out of the fields of Gone with the Wind. Her cotton colored hair tucked neatly in a bun. I noticed her size and her hole-filled stockings and run over shoes. She is maybe 75-years-old. I told her I had some clothes that would fit her and a coat for him, and I would mail it to them. She said, "I could not pay the postage." Seemed I could hear God smile at that. I said, "No, I have friends who help me with postage." I came home and started sorting clothes for the give-away last Saturday and picked her out three pretty "Sunday dresses" that I knew she never had, a pretty all-purpose coat, stockings, sweater, and got him some things. I am mailing them tomorrow. Just no time before then. I have her address if you have a few things – a piece of old used jewelry, stockings or a slip, or something used you no longer need. They are both tall and thin. I suppose she is a 12 and he is a large shirt and pants about 34 waist and length 32 or33. A box of candy for Christmas or some peppermint or a box of cookies, just say Mrs. Cayce told you about them. Address is: Maco and Ernestine ----------------. I just can't imagine what they would do if they got a few packages. I would love to go see where they live. She was very interesting to talk to. The voice of poverty and hard times. Oh! I have heard it so often. It cries out to me in the dark of night, sometimes.

I thank you again with all my heart for your help. I pray for richest blessings upon you and may your holidays be truly joyful and may your charity be returned to you a hundred fold.

Thank You,

JoAnn Cayce

December 26, 1997

Dear Friends,

This time yesterday about 30 miles from here, I was in our big truck handing down two bikes to some very poor little boys with big eyes. I just remarked "These are bikes from Santa's own truck." I was not prepared for what happened. The little 5-year-old screamed, "Is this really from Santa's truck?" He got so excited he started shaking. I looked at him as he mounted the bike, then at the house he lived in, with no smoke coming out the chimney, no wood on the porch and the starving dog tied to the porch. I wondered how their lives could be changed for the better. I wonder this almost every day of my life. It is times like this I wish I had lots of money. I can't ever remember wanting money for money's sake, just for people's sake. They all had colds, running noses and probably ear infections. I only had one coat and not one had on a coat. I felt with the weather so cold, surely if they had a coat they would have it on. I saw no sign there was a Christmas tree in the house. I handed the only child's coat I had down to the little one. The others just had to shiver. I then handed down two big boxes of groceries. They shared the burden of the weight, left the toys sitting in the road and took the groceries in the house. It was Christmas. I had lots of places to go and no time to get a lot of information but marked this location down so I can put it on the list of calls to come back to. This is the way I get "new business" – new problems, new pain, and possibly improve the lives of little children without hope who often, end up someday in the prison system.

This is the Christmas report for 1997. I am also giving those of you who helped me with donations of food, toys, clothes, coats and shoes a big heartfelt, tearful, thank you! To everyone who helped from the least to the greatest from Thanksgiving through the entire month of December, Thank you! It has been truly wonderful what your help did for so many and especially me. In fact, Christmas for families is still going on here. We have continued to be out everyday. Our family Christmas will be tomorrow, the 27th of December. We are still giving away, as calls come in, what you have blessed us to have to give.

We have almost lived at the Armory in Fordyce getting things ready for a give-away almost every weekend from Thanksgiving to the present time. We gave away over 450 boxes of food for Thanksgiving because some of you sent donations. Then the 6th of December had another big clothes give-away. We had boxes of clothes, coats, shoes, household items, etc. come in from all over the United States, and Joannie and I took a week to sort all this. People I had never written to or heard from sent things. It was almost unbelievable the things we had to give-away, far more than any time before. I wish you could have been here to see the pearly gates fly open and the saints come marching in when we opened the Armory doors on Saturday. Over 1,000 ragged, pitiful souls came in. Some took time to hug me as they rushed in. One gave me a terrible cold that has certainly plagued me all of December and of course my asthma kicked in. I also held or hugged the wrong child at this give-a-way and got head lice again. No, I won't say I held the wrong child because those with head lice need hugging the most. But do wish you had been there to see the families rush in, humble, but grinning from ear to ear. I feel greatly blessed to see them helped and so happy. These people have so little. There are some who have more but still cannot afford clothes because of rent, medication, food on their salaries. I let everyone come no matter if they are working. Some are just plain dirt poor as my grandmother used to say. These give-aways are Christmas all year. People are so thankful. This give-away had household, children's, baby's clothes, coats, shoes, curtains, underwear for everybody (which is always so needed), sweaters, socks and wonderful sheets, blankets and a collection of mattresses. What was left we sent to North Arkansas and they had their give-away about the 12th of December and sent word about 800 came.

We left all our tables at the Armory after this give-a-way and on Monday we came back to start working on a food give-away. We went to the Food Bank and for 14¢ a pound we bought three truck loads of food. Your donations helped us buy food for this give-a-way. We gave 562 boxes with about $45 worth of food in each box. We also gave away 1,000 pounds of toilet tissue, 1,000 pounds of disposable diapers, 1,000 pounds of washing powder and Kotex. Watching the people go through the line was a very humbling experience as always.

We had a wonderful surprise. Charlie Pickle was responsible for putting together 9 pick-up truck loads of clothes (to be given away in January 1998), and 1,000 apples, oranges, and hundreds of pounds of candy. They rolled in just before this food give-a-way started on Saturday morning. They worked and helped us give out the boxes of food Joannie and I had sorted for a week to give out. We then all went to the Methodist Church where some young people from that church helped all of us put together nearly 900 stockings filled with fruit, candy, and lots of odds and ends like pencils, pens, key rings and other items. These were given later to two nursing homes, Head Starts, schools, and to all the little children whose names were being turned in who would not have Christmas.

The people helped us with donations during December or we could not have taken care of so many children. Over 600 had Christmas toys, food, candy, fruit, lights, water, treatment for colds, coats, and some got rent paid for the families who were about to be evicted. I bought some children shoes who were practically barefooted or shoes they had were leaking so badly.

Nancy Jewell and a big bunch from Cabot, Arkansas, helped so much by bringing money, food and toys as a group. Two jeeps from Cabot came loaded and they stayed and helped at the toy give-away the week before Christmas. They came and saw how quickly blankets, coats and sweaters can be gobbled up.

The George Martin Sunday School Class of Lakewood United Methodist Church in Little Rock bought and repaired bikes for boys and girls to have for Christmas. It was a wonderful thing for them to do and so much fun to have bikes to give out. Bruce Dantzler delivered them to our big truck parked in Little Rock along with lots of warm clothes, toys, and food.

The Markham Street Baptist Church Senior Singles class in Little Rock gave a big boost with money, toys, clothes, food, shoes and coats to have to give out during the holidays. I can't list all who gave and all who thought of the poor in south Arkansas, but you are all in my heart and prayers. Believe me I know the donations were hard to turn loose of but if you could see and know how much difference they made. I will just list a few differences:

Mary and her disabled husband who had their children put in foster care because they did not have any heat or water will get their utilities turned back on and their children returned because you gave.

Joel and wife's three children had a doctor and antibiotics for their pneumonia (we were told the 1 year old would not have lived through the next day had they not been treated). Later in the week they had a wonderful Christmas, food, and offer of job for the father and rent paid and lights on.

A couple with four little girls got lots of food, clothes, toys because Dr. James Suen and his wife Karen, came from Little Rock with two loaded jeeps. Their family also had rent paid (they were about to be evicted). Your donations also fixed the mother's abscessed tooth. Dr. Suen and wife also helped a family who had nothing for Christmas or to eat. The children exclaimed as the boxes were carried in by the Suens "Oh God, Oh God, Oh God." A family, with two blind children, was also taken care of by the Suens and this was indeed a touching sight.

A man who had no food, coat, shoes or place to stay and to cap this off, had an abscessed tooth was taken care of with your donations.

Turkeys were bought and delivered with your donations. Milk, cookies and canned goods were bought with your last minute donations before Christmas.

Angie Knight came with a load and gave to a family of 16 whose father had been in hospital with very serious problems. The Lowrances came and brought food, toys, clothes to a mother and children who had been deserted by the father.

A lady on kidney machine was helped; an alcoholic was helped and promised treatment. A couple out of drug rehab was set up in an apartment with food, utilities and coats. The future looks bright. We thank you for helping this couple also.

Two nursing homes had parties, filled stockings and in one

nursing home all patients were given a nice gift (used but clean and nice) and had good things to eat because you sent the means. Two Head Starts of poor children had gifts, books, tapes, candy and a party.

One feeding center for senior citizens had gifts. Over and over poor shut-ins were delivered gifts and food. Baby food was carried to babies along with diapers and warm blankets.

December was so busy I hardly saw my husband on our 49th anniversary. It came and went without much fanfare. He bought me 49 long-stem red roses, and I hardly got to enjoy them but no complaints. My husband knows what Decembers are like. He has spent at least 40 of them with me out and running. There were two food give-aways, one used clothing give-away and a huge Christmas give-away during December with many home deliveries and house calls. Because you sent things to give out and donations we just kept running. The jail men had gifts and we hope they will think about this when they reflect on their lives. I know many of them and know how they grew up and the treatment they had. This is no excuse but it does touch me because I felt many would end up in prison. We took care of their children at home.

Many, many children's coats were given out, shoes bought, wood was bought, and one family called at the last minute and said they had just heard about me, and they had to spend the money saved to buy their four children's Christmas for a coffin and funeral for a grandmother who had no burial insurance. They received food and Christmas at the last minute.

The 12-year-old boy who was accused of fathering an 11 year old girl's baby was proven not guilty and a 29 year old man was arrested and charged with rape of the retarded girl. His trial will be January 6th, and again I will go to court on this case. All children involved received Christmas. This case, right at Christmas, was time consuming and caused lots of stress for me while I was trying to give out gifts.

Over 200 dolls were combed, bathed, dressed and looking like new by caring persons and given out to "new mothers" who were so happy to have something to love.

Bessie Mae had a turkey delivered to her little shack the last minute. Midst her tears and hugs she announced to me if she could gather some wood for a fire, they would have Christmas dinner. At six o'clock p.m. another family had a turkey, Christmas toys and blankets delivered and we found what they really wanted was to go to a Christmas service Christmas Eve, but it was so cold and they had no coats. We made a trip home, got coats for all, and they made church and cooked a turkey for Christmas dinner the next day. They had a tree laden with gifts which some of you donated.

Watson's Drug Store in Fordyce had a silent auction, and the benefits came to us to help bail us out in January 1998, because surely by then medication, heat, wood, doctors, teeth and rent will be suffering all over again. My problems with people are never over, but to relieve suffering is the name of the game out here.

This is one Christmas there were no children and mothers thrown out and not one child-abuse case was called in to me during the emergency period. Last year on Christmas Eve one mother called and said she was putting her baby (6 months) in the yard, I could come get it.

Again thank you, each one, who remembered me and my poor. Thank you for the lovely cards of remembrances. Thank you for your prayers.

For the benefit of some who knew I was trying to find the time to cook chili for about 400 for a benefit for children, I did cook 20 gallons of home-made chili and had a wonderful experience. I was in sole charge of the chili and while standing at the big stove in the school kitchen stirring, I turned around and over in a corner saw two cold little children who had just come in. God whispered to me "these children are hungry and have no money." The program was about to start and people were finishing up the deserts and hot, steaming bowls of chili. The dining room was packed. I saw the children looking at the hot bowls of chili as some were in line waiting for seconds. I laid down my stirring spoon and walked over to the children and said, "Do you two want some chili?" The little boy (about 9) held to his sister tight. She was about seven. He said to me with great expression, "That stuff cost money?" I said, "I will pay." They ran to the line, I told the lady taking up tickets. "I'll pay for those two." The next morning at the Post Office I was struggling with 24 boxes of assorted clothing that had come in. I was trying to get them home and open them to see if there were things I needed that day. Someone touched me and said "We will load your packages Mrs. Cayce ... remember we are the ones you gave the chili to last night." Folks, all I could think of was ain't God good?

I love each one of you – for every dime you sent, every ounce of things you mailed, all things you delivered, for the basketball game Mr. Stokes' bunch played to benefit my kids and families; I humbly and with tears, this day, thank you. We will have our Christmas tomorrow. Our family is all here and have been working hard. We are hoping to have a little time for just each other but if that doesn't happen there will be joy anyway. Our thoughts are on all you did to bring so much to so many who were without, until you appeared. May the coming year be your happiest ever. Don't forget I am out here and often with an empty basket.

The phone just rang and an elderly lady said "Mrs. Cayce, when are you having another food give-away, me and my daughter done ate all our food and our checks won't be in for a week." These people are retarded mother and retarded 60-year-old daughter and a big, skinny dog who just can't make it for a whole month. Then a minister called and said a mother, father, and six children were hungry. The father had just got work but won't be paid for two weeks. Don't forget these cases – they are real, and, but for the grace of God, it could be any of us.

Much love,
JoAnn Cayce

September 21, 1998

Dear Friends,

It is so good to finally be able to sit down and write you the story of some of the cases (successes and failures) that have been going on here since you heard from me last. I have not gotten to write all summer, and not a day went by I did not think "you should be here to see and hear this."

I have been working on what I call the Tom and Mary case for months. I found them last Christmas when I took Christmas to their children. I knew it had to be bad from the report I had received about the family. I was loaded with toys, food, warm clothes, blankets, and, sure enough, nothing I had heard was exaggerated. I could tell the father had a terrible muscular problem. He could not walk up his five steps going into the shack they lived in. There was no heat, lights, Christmas tree or water. Human Services took the children a few days later and still have them. I went back time and time again and filed for his disability after I got five doctors to see him free, and all said he had serious problems. Finally Dr. Archer saw him free at UAMS in Little Rock. He said he had degenerative arthritis. He was turned down by Social Security over and over, and I kept appealing. He is in terrible pain. I appealed his case to the Federal level and Wednesday, September 23rd, his case will be heard. Pray for him. He has worked hard since he was five years old in the woods. He has done it all, sawing with a buck saw and later with a chain saw, riding a skidder and loading billets. If I can get an answer quick it will not be too late to get the babies back before they are adopted. Did you know now that there is a certain time parents have to get in position to get their children back, and if they still cannot manage they are put up for adoption? This has its good points and its heart-breaking bad points. I try to see the good in it. Used to be, children were kept in the system for years, back and forth from one home to another. Arkansas needs good foster homes so badly. There are only two foster homes for black children in this part of Arkansas. From what they tell me, they will not cross the color line. This report may not be true. I do know we need foster homes badly. The excuse given me for not picking up children I report is that there is no place to put them (a poor excuse in my humble opinion).

One week a few months ago I reported five abuse cases in one week. I was called on three more that I did not go to the home, just told the person who called me they had to call since they were the witness. Drugs are children's worst enemy. If parents are on drugs, children suffer in ways that are unbelievable. I was called on one dog abuse. The lady was feeding a large dog that never got fed, and the family called the police and accused her of poisoning their dog. The man told the police that he fed the dog and watered it once a month and that was enough. The neighbor wanted me to do something. I have reported it. This dog would make Maxwell look well-fed.

We went through the summer helping baseball kids. Some had no money for shoes, suits and some did not have transportation. We believe it is the right of girls and boys to get to play baseball if they want to. Many do not have the fees, funds for shoes, etc. I have wanted an ice box and a freezer, but every time I plan to buy one "for sure," I see a child with an abscessed tooth or no shoes, or a baby with no diapers, nor formula, and the first thing I know my "freezer money" is gone.

One night, about 8:00, Joannie and I went to several families who were hungry, we knew, and then we headed for the "bad" area where the drug addicts, alcoholics sleep and the homeless often with children, hide in the darkness. When they saw my pickup parked with the doors open, they came from every direction. Soon we had a huge crowd around us. Joannie, who because of her bone deterioration (from cancer treatment) could not get up in the back of the truck with me, had to stand down among the people. She was handing out bags of food as I handed it down. I could tell they were pressing her badly. I finally yelled out, "Move back, we will feed all of you, and we are not afraid of you," (there are no white women I know who would come down here this time of night on Friday night) but you have to be patient". They started yelling, "Mrs. Cayce, you know we would not hurt you, you are the only friend we got." I felt it was necessary to tell them what I did because they were crowding in so fast. "The press of the crowd," as in Jesus' day, is scary. We fed all those who came and some came back for seconds. As we started to get back into the truck, some came around and thanked us over and over. Adults and children went to sleep full that one night. There is hardly a night goes by I don't think of different children I know who I am sure are hungry. We went to a home the other night, Joannie and I, and the children were down in the floor in an empty room with no furniture. When we went in with food, they started clapping their hands and saying "food, food, food." The least one was only two, but she knew what peanut butter, bread, cookies and milk was. Joannie and I both had a cry when we went home. The mother had deserted the children. She is in jail now, and the children are in foster care.

Fordyce Bank and Trust called us on Thursday night. They had fixed too many hot dogs for a pep rally, and they wanted me to bring boxes and come get all that was left. They gave us about 300 hot dogs, still hot, made with huge fine wieners, (not the cheap stuff I am able to buy). My husband went with me (I call him Mr. Wonderful). We went to the jail first, and fed those in jail. This took 56 hot dogs but they were so happy to have a "surprise supper." I had nothing for them to drink but the jailer said, "Don't worry, Mrs. Cayce, they are so happy to get these." They had a canned pop machine but it would have taken lots of quarters. I was as broke as the prisoners were, ha. Then we went to feed families, and finally we fed all the children at the football field who were practicing pee wee football. And the strangest thing happened. As we went in the grounds, a family was walking out. A mother, father and three children. I told Mr. Wonderful to stop. He did, and I said, "Could we give you all a hot hotdog?" They said, "Yes, Mrs. Cayce, and you won't believe this, but the children had just said, 'Oh how they wished they had a hot dog,' and you pulled up." He said, "This is scary." We served them with great joy. I had to call the bank the next day and tell them about that family. We also went down to the homeless and hungry where Joannie and I had gone the week before and Mr. Wonderful stood in the back on the ground as I passed out hotdogs to him. He gave out about 75.

I took a man and wife, very poor, to Little Rock to the doctor, and as I usually do, I took them out to eat. I knew they were hungry, so I took them to a huge buffet. I told them they could eat whatever they wanted and all they wanted – I was buying (with your donations). They got trays, and I went ahead so they would see how it was done, but I told them I had diabetes so I could not eat much, but they could have all they wanted. When they got to the meat area, I said, "Do you want some steak, friend chicken or turkey and dressing?" The man who was right behind me said, "I like all that Mrs. Cayce, I will just have some of all that." Of course, I told the lady who stood in shock behind the counter to give him a serving of the fried chicken, the turkey and dressing, and the chicken fried steak. She repeated it about three times to me and I kept saying, "Yes, some of it all." Then the man's wife said his plate looked good so we went through it all again. They then said one dessert was all they could handle and with a plate of bread and drinks we found a table. If you are not prepared to be stared at, don't take a poor person out to eat, the attention is so great. The lady had on her best – run-over shoes, a print dress with an apron, and a red felt hat that was turned sideways so she could see real well (it was 105 degrees outside) and eye glasses from the 60's (all these things she got at the last clothes give-away, and it was the best she had). I might add, she felt like a million bucks. After having the blessing of being with them all day, I did too. (If you have eye glasses I need them badly.) My poor people come to the give-aways and they try eye glasses on till they can see, and are tickled to death when they find a pair that fits.

If you are filled with vain pride you could never do my job. You have to be cleaned up first. See why I say the poor have done more for me than I have ever done for them. They cleaned me up and taught me what real beauty, love and humbleness is. I often think if I made a video of some of my days and experiences I would win that $10,000 or maybe even that $1,000,000 from the Video show on TV. Then I would take a bus load to the buffet (and maybe win another $10,000).

By the way, this couple never left a crumb. I was almost afraid to walk close to them. I know they were so full they were bound to be explosive but they never said they were "too full." Did you ever think what a luxury it is to be "too full?" Not many people I work with, in fact, I can't think of one who has ever said to me "I am too full."

I have written far too much, and you may have quit on me but there is a book I could write about this summer alone. If you want to make copies of this and carry to your Sunday School Class or send to someone, please do. I would love for your charity to be a blessing to everyone. The Bible says it (charity) is the greatest of all.

Right now, I am facing Thanksgiving and want to give a basket of food to at least 500 needy families. Christmas is just around the corner. We had over 600 children last year who needed fruit, candy, toys, coats and clothes. If you have any used items we can use, help us. If you care enough to mail a check, every dime will be used for a good cause. I'm not begging, I'm giving you the opportunity to "feel great" . . . the greatest of all!

I thank each one of you who helped me. Your checks have performed miracles for so many. A few dollars can literally change the life of an entire family. A little food, diapers, and washing powder will improve a whole family. We have had two big food give-a-ways lately, plus we give away food to several families each day. We have had cereal, juice, medicine for most folks who came. I have purchased a larger van and can carry more, wanted to try to get a grant for a van but there wasn't time and I have been through that before. I decided to do it myself. Again thanks for caring! I believe, with all my heart, we are happier if we reach out and up.

Love You,

JoAnn Cayce

November 22, 1998

Dear Precious Friend,

I would give anything if you could have been with me at the Armory last Friday. We had the Thanksgiving give-away, and it was one of the most touching ones I have ever had. We had advertised the give-away was for the disabled, elderly needing food and the families without work and food. The radio really played up the give-away. They came in wheelchairs, on crutches, walkers and some leading others. Some wanted to reach across the tables and hug me and with tears they told me what the give-away meant to them. One man, big and big sad eyes said he was there because his boss went deer hunting and laid him off for a week. His family had no food and he needed food for his 7 children badly. I gave him two chickens and a big box of groceries and then saw a big bottle of catsup I had bought for discount. I got that and piled it on top. It was just too much for the man, he lost it. When he could control himself he said "My children, just don't get catsup. Thank you with all my heart." We all take catsup for granted don't we? I thought about all those little children with that bottle of catsup. My grandson who lives with us loves catsup on everything, uses a bottle a week. I had such a lump in my throat all day, and that night I could not swallow my supper. I saw so many thin, hungry people so proud of a box of odds and ends, and they could not believe they had a chicken in their box. We have them from 14 to 103 years old. Some had to walk to us and walk home with their boxes. I saw one father leaving toward the end of the give-away, and he was going off down the railroad carrying his box. Some said he could have ridden with them but he was so anxious to get the box home to his children. You know they have cut out so many families who used to be on stamps in the welfare reform now. This reform, I say, reforms folks who have no jobs from can get by to can't get by. They just do without and suffer, and it shows in their faces, eyes, walk and many have just given up

I received your help and want you to know what you sent was greatly appreciated. I had been saving all the money folks sent me (that I did not have to use for emergencies) for the Thanksgiving food. Your checks are now in the bank for the food for Thanksgiving, and if you have been wondering why I had not put them through, it was because if it went in the bank I might spend it, so I saved your checks without cashing them. I was trying to buy all the food I could and get all I could free from different places. Companies just will hardly give food anymore to small charities like mine. They give to big things like Red Cross and such (who spend so much for administrative cost). It is hard to get donations of food, etc. anymore, but I keep trying. I used to get lots of food from folks like Proctor and Gamble, etc. but now they won't contribute. If it were not for folks like you I would be "out of business." I never waste a dime that is given me and I try to work to contribute myself.

So many things have been going on but the main thing was the big food give-away which was Friday. I went to Warren to the Bradly County Helping Hands and got a big assortment the first time and it was about $1,000 worth. Then I went back this last week after I got more donations and got about $500 worth. I went to the Rice Depot in Little Rock and got all they would let me have of rice, odds and ends and cereal. They also let me have 120 bags of meal in 2 ½ pound bags so some of my people could have dressing with their chicken. I also got baby food from the Rice Depot but needed lots more. So many old folks need baby food as they have no teeth. I shopped different places buying salvage as cheap as I could. I shopped at wholesale places. I had a collection from the Boy Scouts in their food drive of about 500 (at least) wonderful canned goods which was what I needed so badly. Tyson was contacted and after many calls and faxing back and forth I was given 500 chickens for the poor. More money came in, and I bought all I could, and we moved everything to the Armory last Monday. I collected boxes from all the beer and whiskey places (it is good that something good can come out of them) grocery stores, alleys and even my drug store, dumpsters, and I went to the dentist with an abscessed tooth (after I had suffered so much I could not stand it and had to stop and go). He had boxes so I loaded them. When you need 500 boxes in a small town it is hard. All in all, we gave way 562 boxes of food and finished them up with chickens so everyone would have a nice fat chicken for Thanksgiving. I got up at 4:15 and went to Tyson in Pine Bluff to pick up the chickens. My people could not believe they had meat in their boxes.

We are having families begging for blankets, coats for children and I am so thankful to Ruby Stewart for sending the young man who mows and does yards a pair of 17 shoes. He was so thankful for the socks. He usually goes without. I am so thankful to the man from Holland who sent the help. I am trying to wait and use his help for coats and food for Christmas. I know Christmas is just around the corner, and I am carrying an empty kettle except for his check. It is wonderful what he did for American families. Thank you with all my heart, Fred. I beg God to grant to you wonderful business and joy and peace and friends. I wanted to go to Washington DC in the hopes of seeing you, but the day the party and presentation was I was giving out food on the 20th. Everyday I am invited to speak or go somewhere; it seems I have something I have to do to relieve suffering.

I want all of you to know I did get my new van. I can carry more people to the doctors and more children to things and families for help. I will be a long time paying for it but my bank is helping me by letting me have the loan at lower interest.

Again know if it were not for my friends helping me I would be lost. I depend on you so much for the help. I get no grants or government help. My husband is retired now, and it is just me. God is greatly depended on. I beg, daily, for Him to touch the hearts of the people who help. My family helps and my kin what they can but I have no wealthy kin, ha.

Please know I love each of you and at 66 I am well and able to put in about 18 hours a day. I have had little sleep at night the last couple of weeks. I had just got to sleep at 4 yesterday morning and got another call. A homeless man was at the motel trying to get to Chicago. He was hitchhiking back home because his 18-year-old son had been killed. He wanted me to pay for him a few hours rest at the motel. Your donations help do all these things. Money for dentist, medicine, insulin, transportation, coats, shoes, school supplies, tapes for Head Starts, refreshments for classes for poor children, blankets, (I was just trying to remember the things you have helped me buy this month) food, gas for big truck to deliver used donation furniture to homes that are bare. One lady cannot get out of her house, has not been able to for over 20 years, and I take her things and see to her. I carried her a donated turkey and food this week, and she loved me, and I see her scared and trembling but she always lets me in. She lets no one else in, cannot bear for folks to get close or come in. I wonder, if I don't stay able to see to her, what she will do. She is so afraid of everyone and everything. I had a doctor to come see her, tested her and told me she was the worst he has seen.

Please pray for all who suffer so. Be thankful for the families who are improving and who we have found jobs for. Many success stories out here. Mothers who have made an inch at a time – are fighting so hard for them to be independent and continue in the schools they are trying to attend and go to work everyday also. They lean on me pretty heavy, but God holds me up. Thank you for being there too. Send me the things you do not want and don't forget toys.

Love,

JoAnn Cayce

January 7, 1999

Dear Friends,

Charity report for Christmas 1998.

Happy New Year! Perhaps you feel like I do – you have been to heaven and back. This Christmas, in fact since the beginning of November, I have been on roller skates – skating from one blessing to another. Every one of you who have given me a thought, a check, a new or used item, those who have mailed packages of toys, clothes, shoes, caps, coats, sweaters I can honestly say from the bottom of my heart THANKS! I often wish you could be with me when they reach the person they were meant for. There is no way it could not humble and touch you. Joannie, my daughter, and I heard about a family who had taken refuge in an old abandoned house in the woods, the day before Christmas. Ice was everywhere and I wondered if we could get over the roads to them. But the report was that they had no food, heat, utilities, beds, Christmas, no way to cook and there were six little children. We packed the van and took off. The temperature was about 24 degrees and we could not imagine not having a fire.

The first trip, we went past the road leading to the house and realized we were getting in deep woods and finally found a little road to turn around but it was covered in solid ice. I knew if we slipped off in the ditch we would freeze to death. I got turned around and went back to the last house we had past and we got directions but no one believed there was a family "down the road." When we found the house it was about a fourth of a mile off the little road. We could see it in the middle of the trees and solid ice and frozen mud. I knew we would have to "walk in." My daughter is disabled so I told her to stay in the van and I would take one load at a time. She insisted on coming with the first load. We got half way to the house and the man and woman came running out (she was barefooted). She was screaming "Mrs. Cayce, Mrs. Cayce". I did not know her, but she knew me and was tickled to death. They had put together an old heater and had a small fire in one lean-to room at the back. We had lots of canned goods, cereal, crackers, soup, canned meat, fruit, candy, cookies and bread but they had no can opener, pans, plates, spoons but I tried to think of all the things we had brought and not focus on what they or we did not have. They were so happy to have food and things for the little children for Christmas. They had no water, and I wished we had brought more juice. The children were thirsty of course. The man does have a job but with the weather like it is he could not work. The job he had, which was what most have, was a woods job.

I found out they could get lights turned on for $100. I made out a check to Ouachita Rural Electric but after we left I thought "how will they get to the office 30 miles away to turn in the deposit and sign up for a hook up?" They had told me they were renting but got behind with all the rain we had had and the man put them out. This old house belonged to kin of the daddy so they moved in. No one had been there for years so it was just a shack with no utilities. It will take many trips and money to get the house piped for gas, water and get them some beds and more blankets. I had one for each child with me the first visit that had just came in from Texas. Also some caps, gloves from Pennsylvania and in another box mailed in were some jackets, socks from New York and Missouri, and, from Illinois some warm clothing. I wondered, as we started back through the woods with the trees loaded with ice, how could these people survive in that cold house?

But before all the home deliveries started and the emergency runs started, we were at the National Guard Armory. This was the day we were to give out Christmas to parents for their children. This was the 18th of December. It was our 50th Wedding Anniversary. We were to have a big party but had called it off. There was no way I could do both, party and Christmas. Our family agreed with us; we all knew what we had to do. We had to provide Christmas and help families.

We had wonderful warm coats, caps, gloves, shoes, clothes, toys, dolls (with new hairdos, clothes and a bath). Names of needy children had come in from agencies, schools, churches, neighbors, families, DHS offices, and kinfolks. For 10 days, Joannie and I had packed trash bags for each child. My daughter Kandy and son-in-law Ted from Little Rock had bought bright green, thick, large trash bags and they looked so pretty stuffed for children with all kinds of goodies.

Some folks in Illinois had prepared 800 stockings with all kinds of things like candy, fruit, and pencils for children. We also had a party on the 18th for nursing homes and Senior Citizen groups and gave them a stocking as well as a gift. School students and Boy Scouts helped with all this, and the elderly in nursing homes loved having the youngsters come see them loaded with Christmas. We want to thank each one of you who helped provide items for everyone. Warm sweaters, blankets, shirts, house shoes, warm up suits. We want to thank the many young people who helped wrap gifts. This means so much. I could never have done this alone.

Dr. James Suen and son, Bradly, came from Little Rock and brought Christian to 3 families and were such a help to us by bringing a blazer with many extra toys, clothes, shoes and food.

My daughter Joannie helps me too, but her ability is limited. Many hours were spent accomplishing Christmas for many who would not have had any otherwise. I sure do have more admiration for good old Santa! This year was a record of children and families needing our help. At last count, there were 756 little children who had received Christmas and about 350 families received food and had serious needs met.

All of November with the Thanksgiving food give-away and clothes give-away folks were also coming needing doctors, medication, help for this or that. Things kept going on (like always) that would break your heart. On Christmas Day we were trying to deliver the last of Christmas and trying to take care of everyone who came to the porch (front and back). One young woman came who had been beaten up. She was seven months pregnant. When the husband started beating her she rolled over on her stomach to protect her unborn, and he hit her all over the back. She had to have medical attention. Another mother with a 5-month-old had no food for her baby. She came, and she had two black eyes and was beat up all over. She wanted diapers, formula, baby food and food for herself. Another pitiful case a 13-year-old came wanting Christmas for herself and her 7-month-old baby. They needed everything. This was a rape case and the father of the baby was in jail. It is hard to celebrate sweet Jesus when you see so much pain and suffering, but what if He had not been born?

We had a young father come who had just found a job, but he needed a tank of butane for heat, some food, and he needed shoes for his feet. I gave him some boots someone had given me. He was so tickled. I took him over to the warehouse and was getting him some food but he kept looking around. I did not know what he saw he wanted, but as we started putting food in his old car he looked at me with tears and said "Mrs. Cayce, I saw a coat that would fit my wife and she has none, and I saw an old rocking chair. You've been so good, but could I have those two things?" I said, "Yes, let's go back in and see." I don't know how he had seen the old rocker with so much piled on it but I told him if he could get it out he could have it. It was freezing cold and solid ice and sleet outside. He worked pulling the rocker out. He was grinning from ear to ear. He said, "My wife and I have wanted a rocker since the baby came. We wanted to rock him, but we didn't have a rocker. I will fix this one up." I want to tell the people who left it on the warehouse porch, thanks. It was a wonderful Christmas blessing to that little baby, his 16-year-old mother, and 19-year-old father. The daddy said, "I never thought we would get food, butane, coat for my wife, rocker, food and diapers for my son and me a pair of boots. This is sure a good Christmas. I thought of that saying, "A man's wealth is measured by his needs."

We had our family Christmas after Christmas and decided against the 50th Wedding Anniversary party. Our family had done so much to help us. And every one of you, my dear friends, who have helped me in 1998, I appreciate you. I am still out here because you have put something in my hands to work with. You can't give much out of an empty basket. 1999 is facing me and I am facing you, hoping you will not forget me and the people who depend on us when they are against the wall. Winter is upon us and cold hurts. I know, yesterday I was out most of the day in 18 degree weather and in several houses it seemed it was warmer outside than inside. I wished for a van load of blankets but I have learned to work with what I have. I thank you for coming through in 1998. I thank God when something comes in that I need badly: money for medicine, food, boots, baby clothes, shoes, coats, blankets. May God bless you and give you what you and I need, I pray.

Love,

JoAnn Cayce

May 19, 1999

Dear Friend,

I have set aside today (it wasn't easy) to write you the news. It is a treat (to me) to get to do this.

I wanted to tell you about the Easter party. It was moved to the City Park in Fordyce, Arkansas, about five miles from Thornton. It just kept getting larger and larger. We had over two hundred children from all ages and backgrounds. One young couple came and brought their two children – cute little ragged, scrubbed clean, smiling children about two and three. The daddy told me they would have no Easter and saw in the paper about the hunt. He said, "This is it for my children, can we all stay?" Of course I said, "Yes." I pointed to a bush not far away and said, "When the bell rings to start take them to those bushes, there is two big stuffed gray bunnies hidden inside." I know now what the Clearing House sweepstakes winners look like first hand. His children were screaming with delight and he and his wife were crying they were so happy. They said a big "Thank you." I guess this might have not been 100% fair but I had to do it. It is doubtful these two kids had ever had a stuffed toy before. Later you should have seen this family eat. The children were stuffing it in with both little hands.

Joannie and I with volunteer women hid over 1,000 eggs, stuffed toys, other toys folks had donated, all over the park. We had several who had sent in donations and ask that this be put in eggs for the children to find. So we put $1 bills in plastic eggs, and three had $5 inside. Joannie had bought some golden eggs for the money. I wish I could have had 1,000 eggs with $1 inside. When they found a $1 egg you would have thought there was a fire and this was the siren. We had everything good to eat after the egg hunt. This was spread on picnic tables and they were allowed to form lines and get all they wanted. We had Little Debbie's, punch, cake, ice cream, sandwiches, candy, cookies, eggs, and fruit. One beautiful blonde, blue eyed little boy kept coming back and back getting tray, and tray loaded... leaving and returning. I decided to follow him, busy as I was. He was going a van loaded with tiny children. The lady driving said they were all sick but wanted to come so badly. The blonde boy was well and was the runner. He was about five. She was a foster mom, she said. I went back and got boxes of goodies and brought them back to the van, I don't know if this is where I got it but the next day I was sick as a dog. At the park there was so much room and it was easier to watch so many. Also there was all kinds of play equipment. I want to thank those who mailed bunnies, candy, plastic eggs, money for the eggs, and decorations. Thanks to the Little Debbie Company, all of the stores who gave food of all kinds and certainly for the volunteers who helped hide and keep herd on the children. My causes are not usually blessed with volunteers and are often so heart breaking no one can stand to volunteer more than once a year or so. When we have wonderful people to turn out and help, it is so special to us.

We had a tremendous clothes give-away two weeks after the egg hunt. In fact we went to work on Monday after the egg hunt party to get the clothes give-away ready. We could not have it in the National Guard Armory as we have for all of 23 years because the bombing abroad had started and the guard was on call. We were trying to get out clothes for children to finish school in and getting calls constantly asking for cooler clothes. There was a big old vacant gym in Fordyce where the old high school used to be. We got permission to use it. When I walked in I almost gave up on first sight. I am too old to clean a gym, and I knew I was heading for an asthma field day. We had no tables, brooms, rest rooms, water-fountains, phones or good way to back up trucks for unloading. We had, to go up steps to get in with heavy boxes of clothes. There were no fans for cooling, and it had just turned hot. I went up on stage, looking out over the mess of pop cans, paper, discarded school books, computers, gym equipment which was too heavy for me to move, and I had to give myself a good kick and play the glad game. I did have tons and tons of good clothing, shoes and household goods, and I remembered when I didn't have anything to give away and had stood amidst NOTHING. So I rolled up my sleeves and with Joannie's help and one faithful worker (that I pay) we started hauling off all the junk gathered there in the years it had not been used. It took ten days to move the clothes after the gym was cleaned and sort all the "stuff." We had the biggest clothes give-away in our history. Tons of school clothes were given to children trying to finish the school year. We might have had 1,000 pairs of shorts and shoes. I stood back and watched them pour in on Saturday, and it must be like the Pearly gates flying open. The crowd was so big someone called the police to control the crowd out side and the traffic. They took away hundreds of filled trash bags. Everyone was so happy. I took care of as many children as I could while parents grabbed clothing. The crowd was close to 1,000 I am sure, maybe more. A wonderful success! Thanks to everyone who mailed in the least thing. What was left was carried to Sparkman, Arkansas, where there again, we had many poor hungry and anxious people waiting. We added more to the leftovers and had another big give-away.

As soon as the clothes give-a-way was over I started gathering food and getting folks to the doctor and seeing about all the calls that had come in while I was sorting the clothes. We had the food give-away last Saturday on the 15th and, after filling boxes for over a week and moving them to the warehouse, we started at 10:00 a.m. The street was shut off and lines started a little after 7:00 a.m. We had elderly, crippled, homeless, disabled of all kinds, single moms, families without jobs, down on their luck, lined up. We had smoked sausage, 800 loaves of bread, whole chickens, wieners, 6 to 8 cans of food for each box, sugar, flour, meal, oil, two boxes of cereal for each box, rice, beans, crackers, chili, catsup, jelly, peanut butter, cookies and cakes, and juice in their boxes. This was one of the biggest food give-aways we had ever had. One fellow came up to me and just broke my heart. He looked at me and with tears rolling he said, "Mrs. Cayce, you have come far. I remember when all you had to give away were a few cans of beans and bread and a big smile." Looking into this dear man's face, I dared not think that this give-a-way left me $19.45 in my charity bank account. I do not know how I will manage the medicine, doctors trips, and even the poor phone bill much less all the children who need things next week for the closing of school, but I have operated by faith all these years, and I know God will "see us through."

This week is award week at the schools, and I want Bruce Dantzler and his friends to know the bikes they fixed were given (all but one) to children who had none but had been good and read lots of books. There were 7 bikes but one was given to a little boy I met along the way a week ago, I was going to the post office and I saw this little boy with raggedy shoes more off his feet than on, torn jeans and an arm load of books. I stopped and talked to him. He said he loved to read and lived over yonder in that trailer with his "uncle." He said he was from Las Vegas. I started checking on him and found his mother was a street-walking druggie in Las Vegas and he was sent here to live with his mother's family, who did not want him. A man he calls his "uncle" took him in and soon the man got hurt in the woods and is not getting to work. The boy is 11 and on the streets except when he is in the library reading. He walks everywhere because he had no bike. I went after him, gave him food and showed him the bikes. He kept wiping his eyes and his nose as he looked at each one. I ask him about his shoes and he said his were fine. I ask him if his uncle was good to him. He kept looking at the bikes and said, "He gave me half of his Snicker bar, and he shares his food." So in this he judged his "uncle" was good to him. I put his foot down on a piece of paper and marked it. He rode his new bike off. When the charity bank balance comes up I will take the paper and get him some shoes to finish out school. He is riding his bike over town and most days he comes to see me. Of course I am always hard to find. He needs everything – soap, toothpaste, brush, shirts, jeans, socks, underwear. I think a 14 will fit him or 16. He did not get to come to the clothes give-away. He watches and cares for himself. He loves the library. He said he is cool there, and it is quiet, and he knows where all his favorite books are. I imagine he has been on the streets all his life and looking out for himself. This summer he will be like many children, eating what he can find and what people give him. Of course I stay on the move looking for children I know take care of themselves and have little to eat in the summer. In summer in rural areas there are no summer feeding programs.

The school in Fordyce called me last week. They said there was a new family come to town from Michigan. The children were brought to school with only the clothes on their backs. They had no food, car broke down, no furniture, money or place to live. Would I go see about them? Of course the first thing I thought about was there was no money in my charity bank account, and I had really been straining my own funds: Could I take on another family? Then the age old question, "Could I not do it?" I thought about what the poor man said when he gave me $20 to help buy chickens for the food give-away, "Mrs. Cayce, most people say they do not have it to give, and I don't either, but not having it to give is no excuse," as he handed me $20. I said, "Out of your own need you have given, and I believe God recognizes this more. Having "no money in the bank" is not an excuse for me to not take on another family. I went to where they were staying. It was an empty, dirty, bare, trailer. I had two pairs of used tennis shoes in my van and some jeans and shirts, and tooth paste. One of the boys is mentally ill and was being committed the next day, He was so precious, loving and lost is the best way to describe him. He is 10. He grabbed one of the pairs of tennis shoes and they fit him perfect. One boy is 15, is over six foot tall and wears size 18 men's shoes. He needs everything and has been washing his jeans (he said) in a lady's yard with her hose at night. I had tooth paste but no brushes in my van. When I said I have no brushes but maybe they could use clean rags until some tooth brushes came in. "We ain't got no rags, we don't brush anyway," said the 3rd. grader. I said, "Well you are going to start." I gave them the boxes of food left over from my food give-away, and they grabbed the cereal and started eating it dry. The mother and step-dad said they all had eaten that day at the school. The mother swelled very badly and her face all covered with blisters. I thought about Lupus, diabetes and aids. This will be a long and hard job and the school is depending on me working a miracle. I have been gathering this family things all week, except yesterday I had to drive to Texarkana to accept the Blue Cross, Blue Shield award as their Community Volunteer for Arkansas. (As they handed me the plaque I was thinking, "I bet the motel would let me bring this family in for a couple hours and let them all bathe tonight" (Never thought I'd rent motel rooms by the hour.)

I know this is too long but I want you to know how much I depend on you, and at this time I need each of you to say a prayer and reach out (if possible) to my people. I really need some help. I will try to be more careful this summer and not get in such a tight. I have not wasted a dime, I have also supported my causes too and certainly have not taken advantage of any help given. So many things come up unexpected for example: a senior young man, who I had to remove from his violent home and find him a place to stay for two months so he could just finish high school next week, needed $20 to go to try out for a choral scholarship. He had a ride but I had to buy the gas. Then another in almost the same situation wanted to go on the trip to Hot Springs with his classmates needed $40 to go. He has a job for Saturday, and he can pay me back but he needed it for today. I am so proud of his grades, when he had taken beatings and cussing all year because he would not stop and "get a job." He stuck with school, I thought my $40 was well spent, even if I do not get it back, but I believe I will. I wish all of you and the teachers knew what some of these kids go through just to get to attend classes and take part in some of the activities. I had to put one up in a motel one night just so he could study. There was so much drunkenness in the home he could not study for a test. Life comes hard for some of the young folks, and they have no one to complain to that they can trust. Together we have worked out many problems this year. Seems it is harder for kids who want to do right these days because their families are so dysfunctional. I think, really, they deserve credit as well as kids who have security and so many advantages such as the love of a family. Like one young man who hugged me at the prom I was invited to attend a week ago. He said, "Mrs. Cayce, I did the best I could because I knew you cared."

I know some of the things I do for kids seem small, but if it keeps a child in school or encourages them in even a small way I think it deserves my efforts. When a young person has love and the help, cooperation, and security of a family to excel this is wonderful, but for those who have nothing, no one, not a dime, to even stay in school, they need a big hand.

There is a picnic going on today for the poor children in several of our Head Starts. It is a cookout. A few boxes of wieners, buns, cookies, candy and drinks, relish and mustard, is giving kids a hand-up for a day and making them feel loved and happy. I will be going over to have a look at their faces. I have seen them cry so often, I want to see their laughter and rejoice. Their party cost me so little compared to the return. Think of me and my people, please. I am saying for the first time, I can remember: I need your donations if your heart allows.

Love,
JoAnn Cayce

September 23, 1999

Dear Friends,

I promised I would try to get a charity report off this week. It has been sometime since I wrote my wonderful friends and let you know what is going on.

We did get all the poor kids in school. Some aren't shod the best, but their feet are covered. I am still working on supplies, notebooks, milk and lunch money, socks, and underwear. Bare behinds are also a problem. Also the little school here that is K to 4 needs paper towels, Kleenex, some patent medication such as aspirin and non-aspirin, bandages, first aid items. No, there is no money in our little school for that. I try to take a load of supplies over several times a year. They also need Rid (head lice treatment) shampoo and soap and hand soap.

Speaking of head lice I had an experience with this yesterday. There is a new family moved in from Georgia. The real father died several years ago when his brain exploded. This is what his little girl told me. The step-father of several months is a deaf mute but able to work and has gotten a job in the few weeks they have been here. I think he is a nice man. I heard about this family from someone who cared and came by and ask that I check on them. He said they were very poor. That was an understatement. I will take you through this case because many of you have asked, "Where do you find the poor." When I heard about this family I was having clothes give-away the next day (last Friday). I went down, and they said they had a way and would be there. They live about nine miles from here, and the children are in the school where I am on the school board. The family came to the Armory where the give-away was held on Friday. They were very, very dirty. They had no water on. There were two girls in the family, 10 and 15. The ten-year-old was nearly blind but sharp as a tack. She set out at once looking for shoes for the entire family. They were barefooted. She is thin, blonde with blue eyes and beautiful. She needed no help.

There were over 500 people at the give-away. It was hard to get around. We had lots of Mexican people who did not speak English. I was having to handle this. There were also families who had never been to a give-away before. Joannie and I hold babies and watch children. We had one two year old that got lost, and this was a very scary time. Finally she was found in the car. She had gotten out of the building and gone to her car, gotten in and gone to sleep in the hot car. Everyone was so happy she was found.

This give-away furnished lots of linens and blankets. Many were grabbing these. Our most needed items are household. We also had lots of used mattresses. I had five volunteers working, and I had hired two strong men to help with the lifting. Of course Joannie and I tried to be everywhere.

The new family left with clothes for everyone, and Kristin, age 10, had gotten shoes for everyone but the mother. She wears size 11 and there were no women's shoes that large. I looked at her dirty feet and could tell she was used to being barefooted. But she had a big smile and happy they had gotten so many needed items. I promised the mother I would see about glasses for Kristin the next day. The teacher had already told me the child was brilliant but nearly blind. She moved her up on the front seat hoping that would help her see.

On Monday I called a doctor in Camden to see about glasses for the child, and he said have her there at 3:30 p.m. I went down to pick up the child but she was not at the school. They had sent her home. I was not told why. I went to the shack they lived in and found they were packing, had been put out. The place was shut down for repairs. They had no place to go. I told them to pack and I would take the child to the doctor and be back as soon as I could (I did not get back until 6:30 p.m.). On the 18-mile trip to the doctor the little girl told me all their belongings had been lost when their house had flooded in Georgia. She also told me about her father's brain "exploding." She seemed so happy to have someone to talk to. She told me a lady in the lunch kitchen at her new school invited her to church and told her she would come for her. She was so trilled about that. She had gone to church twice. Kristin also told me about finding a dress for her mother at my clothes give-away on Friday before. She hoped her mother would wear it and go to church next Sunday. She said it has been a long time since her mother had a pretty dress and could go to church. Kristin started describing the dress. She said: "Mrs. JoAnn, you know some dresses have those plastic diamonds on them." I said, "Yes." She said, "Well this dress does not have plastic diamonds it has the real diamonds all over the top." I thought about her mother having no shoes and dirty feet. But folks, if you had been there you would never have laughed or thought what she said funny, I promise you. It broke my heart. I could just see her mother (like Kristin) in a dress with real diamonds looking so pretty (in spite of dirty bare feet). I asked her if she found a dress for her 15-year-old sister to wear, and would she go to church too. Kristen said, "Mrs. JoAnn, she is not holy like my mother and me, so she would never go to church." I ask if she had rather stay home and watch TV (see folks, I forget too). Kristen said, "Mrs. JoAnn, we don't have no TV."

All the way to the doctor I got lessons in poverty from the mouth of a child who accepts it and has no complaints. I was almost to the doctor's office when I said "Why did you get sent home from school today, were you sick?" She said so naturally "No, the nurse found I got the head lice, but not bad, just a little bit (in case you don't know lice doesn't come in small batches) We don't have any money for medicine. Do you mind?" (She was afraid she would lose a friend.) I said, "Listen, as soon as we finish getting your glasses we will go to Wal-Mart and get some medication for the whole family and we will take care of this problem tonight." She gave me a 100 yard smile.

The doctor said she was almost blind, in the left eye and her sight very bad in the right eye. The nurse helped her pick out the latest in glasses, and they looked great, but it would have been hard to make this beauty look anything but great – lice, dirt and all couldn't do that! It was hard to listen to her pitiful tales for praying about the last one she told. I knew they were all true because of the simple way she told them. She didn't want pity, she just wanted to "tell somebody." She described her father's death, no food, the flood, no coat, not being able to see, her mother only getting $400 a month Social Security, and on and on.

Reminded me of the time I took the poor, old lady to the doctor and then out to eat and in the middle of the restaurant she stopped to twist and tie her cotton stockings in a knot and turn them under to hold. It was so natural and simple it was not even noticeable to her.

When we left the doctor's office this beautiful child stepped outside in the light with her new glasses on, and looked up at the trees, then the flowers around his building and across the street and gave the world a million dollar smile. She didn't have to say "Isn't the world a beautiful place?" I knew what she was thinking and feeling! I don't know if she has ever seen the beauty of her surroundings before. Man! the education I get out here. I'd hate to have to pay the tuition. I couldn't.

So friends, put your thumbs in your suspenders and rare back. Your donations bought the gas to take her to the doctor, bought the head lice treatment for the entire family, their supper, her glasses and gave her a life. Because of your donations this past week, she is able to see and now can get an education, not be teased, in fact, you changed her whole life. As she said, she did get real diamonds!

This is just one family. Since I wrote you there are so many. One in Sparkman whose house burned and the mother is in Children's Hospital, critical. The four children have no clothes, shoes, and we have gathered clothes to take there tomorrow. One husband who beat his wife has repented and the family is doing lots better. A 15-year-old has a home for herself and her newborn infant, a mother and three children have gotten a safe place and job for the mother. Food has been given to over 96 families during August, and many children were fed during the summer.

This clothes give-away touched one life that is changed forever. This lady is well off and volunteered to work in the give-away. After it was over she came to see me the next day and said when she started to leave the give-away on Friday when it was over, she noticed two elderly sisters waiting with lots of trash bags of belongings they had gotten at the give-away. They had walked and by faith they waited, praying someone would give them a ride home. This wealthy lady in her big car invited the sisters to ride. She said, she told them she would take them home. They loaded all their bags and were beside themselves with joy to ride in the fancy car and have a free ride home. They gave directions and the lady said, "When we got there it was just a shack, without even much of a roof, and I helped them get in the house, but they had no chest to put things in or any furniture or chairs but they were so happy and tickled to have all the things they had gotten. You would have thought they lived in a mansion." She continued with tears, "JoAnn, this was one of the best things that has ever happened to me. I went home and looked at all my beautiful furniture and really saw for the first time, what I had. Those poor sisters have nothing and were thankful – they changed my life."

Dear friends, that is what doing for others does for you. It opens your eyes and teaches you to share. What is more important in life than this? Thank each one of you who have helped me. Be it boxes, packages, food, money, encouragement. It all means so much. What you send is used to bless someone and relieve suffering. The teachers tell me when I have had a give-away, the kids come to school the next week so proud of all their "new" things. I take what you give and turn it into self esteem, pride and pure joy. Doesn't that make you proud? I could never do it without you. The medicine you help buy, the dentist or eye glasses for a child. A human being suffers with a tooth ache that has to hurt until it bursts. Can you think of anything you had rather do than stop the pain? I can't!

I love you all. I am working on Thanksgiving and Christmas. If you have good, used toys or food or a few extra dollars, used clothes or household items. I am not begging, I am giving you an opportunity for the best medicine for happiness in the world!! Charity.

Sincerely,
JoAnn and Joannie Cayce

December 29, 1999

Dear Friends and Supporters,

I wish I could hug each one of you today and tell you with the tears that are falling how much your love and support means to me. Christmas is past, I am broke, people are still in need and I wonder if the Band Aids I am able to provide will hold back the blood. But I am comforted by the fact some of you are calling and writing already asking "what are the needs now?" Thank you each, for the things you sent, checks, packages, fruit and hundreds of items we gave out. If it had not been for you there would have been nothing in Santa's bag.

On the 13th of December, we moved 3 big trucks of used toys and bikes to the National Guard Armory in Fordyce. At that time we had almost 500 children's names on the list and it didn't take a Master's Degree to know we were very short on new items, items for eleven, twelve, and teenagers. There were Barbies without clothes and bikes with no air. When I came home that afternoon I was a little down, but it didn't last long, boxes were stacked on our front porch from the post office, UPS and American Express from Pennsylvania. Marcia Bonk had mailed boxes of new cars and toys for boys and dolls for girls – only new toys were opened. There was a call from Pam Galloway telling me she had about 500 warm coats for children. A letter from Bruce Dantzler telling me he had bikes, the McCarrisons remembered poor, cold little children with boxes to fill many needs. I can't list everyone, but all of your names are before me today. It was truly wonderful. My spirits were lifted to Glory! Everyday it seemed our cries were heard. Food was shipped in; the very thing I wished for, someone sent or brought.

Dr. James Suen family, including his wife, Karen and son Brandon, from Little Rock came with a jeep and U-Haul trailer filled with the needs for several families. Jerry Atchley and wife contributed to this effort also. They had an assortment of basketballs, bikes, food, clothes, coats, blankets and bedding.

Just when I was giving out, a new burst of energy and supplies showed me there was a tremendous effort behind this besides me and my family.

I took an armload of coats one night to a family. I was so beat from the day at the Armory but this family had no heat and the father was sick. As I slipped a coat on the little four-year-old boy he looked up at me and said, "Feels good." I felt his shivering body and saw him pull it close with unbelieving eyes that it was actually his. I was overcome. My children used to say, "Momma is a tester to see how many times a heart will break and keep on ticking." How can we not all share a coat, a blanket, a pair of shoes that will ease the suffering of a child who is cold, hungry or hurting?

I had to stop and come back to this. I will tell you what I stopped for. It is noon on Wednesday after Christmas. A 16-year-old girl came with a neighbor who brought her. He said I fed him back when he lost his job and "saved his life." So when these people moved in down the road and had so many needs, he thought of me. The young lady said her mother was hurting so bad in her neck she had to stop her job. She has hurt about five months. She has no money, no insurance, and does not know what causes the pain. The daddy took the easy way out (he walked), and they have run out of food, no utilities, cold and no blankets. She and the man who brought her were here without coats. I gave them a coat and a warm sweater some of you mailed in. The young girl said, "Mrs. Cayce, do you mind if I give this coat to my brother, he is 14 and ain't got none." I said, "Well let me find him one." I did, a nice used coat and she started to cry. I noticed she had no tears coming from one eye and it was stuck shut. I ask her if she had an artificial eye and she said, "Yes, but I ain't had no money to get me no eye drops, and my eye sticks to my lid cause it is so dry." I had fixed three boxes and two bags of food and picked out an assortment of clothes. I told her to come home with me and I would call the drug store and arrange for her to have drops and charge to my charity account. They left with food for her family and the neighbor man who brought her out of his own need. His car was a wreck and he was too. He said he got laid off in November until after Christmas and was "just trying to make it."

They have gone now and the happiness in their faces is a sweet memory, and I will try to get back to the Christmas report. We had more volunteers this year to help at the Armory than ever before. After we had put everything we had in bags for children the Bradley County Helping Hands called and said they had a load of toys come in, and for $500 we could buy them all. They were not charging us for the toys, only the shipping. I looked up and said, "Lord you are truly the greatest miracle worker. We had received four $100 donations that morning and three $50 donations, so I would say He is a good bookkeeper too! We fixed bags all the next day with these toys but that evening Human Services sent a message that they had 42 families' applications for Christmas, and no one had picked any up. These had 122 children. The school sent us a list of about 31 children, and the jail called and asked if we could take the children who would have no Christmas because the parent was in jail. My husband's office was turned into Santa's workshop that night and we made bags of toys for children most of the night with packages on our porch when we came in. When I got in that night, Toys For Tots had a message on my answering machine that I had an assortment waiting for me in Little Rock. My husband and I went the next night to get these. Our old truck broke down on the way home. We did not either one say "why now?" because a man in another truck pushed us. Later we stopped at the Subway sandwich out of Little Rock on Dixon Road and ate for the first time that day. We left our motor running and enjoyed the bright moon light and talking about our 51st Wedding Anniversary in two days. We got home loaded with toys, knowing how Santa must feel when he gets back home.

Every time I ran out of "stuff," your check or package would come in or someone would call. Even on Thursday before we gave out the bags on Friday a group from Illinois came with blankets, 800 stockings with candy and fruit, and they brought food bags. By then we had over 750 names of children who would have no Christmas without our efforts.

In a newspaper article a year or so ago someone was quoted as saying my causes never stop, they just kept going on and they did day planned, and it did not include looking for folks in the woods on the ice, but then my plans are made to be broken. I was going to deliver bikes that had just come in for the past three days, and God just opened up the world to us. There were some big boxes filled with all kinds of toys, blankets with pictures of animals and warmth. I cried all the way back to the office where we had our meager leftovers stored where it was warm. It was so wonderful. We opened them and Joannie talked about them being delayed in shipment. I said, "Well it came in God's own good time." This was just what we needed for the Santa run to the family just called in. We packed food, toys, some balls that came in, coloring books and colors, and then got some used shoes, etc., then over the ice my daughter and I went. We were packed. We went past the road first then turned back and found it at the end of a wooded road. We saw it off the road, pitiful house almost falling down and only a tiny bit of smoke from a lean-to back room. We started taking armloads over the solid ice, slipping and sliding. My daughter is disabled, and I told her to put hers down and I would come back for another load. About that time the mother and daddy saw us...it was getting darkish. They called for us not to try to make it to put it down and they would come for it. They knew me and started shouting, "Mrs. Cayce, Mrs. Cayce." They were crying, and she was barefooted. I never saw such happy people when they had nothing to be happy about. I told them I would get their lights on, gave them a check for $100 made out to the electric company, but no way to get it on for Christmas. They had fixed up an old wood heater and had a fire in one room. The house had not been stayed in in a very long time. I knew they did not have dishes, can opener or anyway to heat the canned goods. I knew we had to go back later. We were like throwing a feather at a bull in our visit but they were so happy to see us. No transportation. There was a church near and I told them to go see if they could get water at the church. A neighbor said they could get a bath at her house, and I feel she will get some water. I am going back tomorrow again to take things and see about them. The father has a job in the woods but the weather is so bad he could not work and got laid off and the man renting to them put them out on the street. I just wanted you to know that little cold bodies are wrapped in blankets and little dirty hands are playing with toys, and your thoughtfulness in sending money to help or boxes of toys and clothes gave us all the things we were pleased to buy or unpack. Many things God gave us through your being mindful of poor people and little children is so touching to me. I know God is concerned about the people here or he would not have moved you to do something for them. He has to be aware and touch you or you would not have sent these things. Thanks for everything you have ever done and especially lately. I will send out a charity letter next week.

I have had something like a blood clot and had to go to the hospital but found it was a pulled tendon from over use. "In seven hours," I said, "I got to get out of here." Days I got no rest, and I suppose my legs on concrete just gave out. But I never did have to "give up" and am going strong. I am so thankful...this is the time of the year I need every minute. Weather is so bad and people suffering so much. My pain is better. It was worth it all.

I love you,

JoAnn Cayce

June 9, 2000

Dear Friends,

I promised some of you I would mail this letter last week but due to so many unexpected problems I did not get to, but today I have much to rejoice about so it might be best I am writing this week.

I had a little 14-year-old boy who is somewhat retarded or slow, and his mother took on a boyfriend. I think the boyfriend came simply because the child got an SSI check, and he wanted it. The chubby child has lost almost 36 pounds since the boyfriend moved in, and he stayed beaten up (busted lip, cut arm, hurt leg) all the time. The man would not let the child eat much at the table. He told his aunt, and the loss of weight testified the boy was telling the truth. But, because we had not seen the licks and the food abuse, the hot line for child abuse said nothing could be done. Today after three days of working with Social Security, Human Service and others this child was taken from the boyfriend and his mother and given custody to the aunt. I have just received word and am so happy the child will have a good supper tonight and some new clothes. He has had only rags to wear.

I want to start farther back, however, and tell you about Easter. Thank all who gave baskets, plastic eggs, rabbits, candy and little shoes and dresses for the little girls to wear for Easter. Our party was at the park and there were over 300 parents and children. We hid 2,500 fake eggs and 100 real eggs and a lot of eggs had money inside thanks to Mitz Mosier and the Homemakers Club in Sherwood, AR. One man sent some five dollar bills to be put in eggs and did not want his name used. One little shy, poor girl only found two eggs because she was not aggressive and mostly stood still but one of her eggs had a five dollar bill in it. The child cried she was so happy. She said she was going to buy her Momma and brother a present. Some of you sent money for food to be served. Serve we did! We had 6 gallons of ice cream, 12 cases of little Debbie's, candy bars, eggs, 5 gallons strawberry drink sent from Pittsburgh by Nicky Roy, 4 gallons Coke and four gallons root beer and Orange Crush. We hung your rabbits and stuffed animals on trees and in bushes, and baskets were hidden packed full. Screams filled the air as these were found. We gave away 200 filled baskets to those five and under, and all had a rabbit, or stuffed toy inside. This party was the best ever and thanks for every consideration mailed in or dropped on our porch. It was suppose to rain that Friday we had the party but we prayed and prayed and the afternoon was perfectly beautiful.

We want to report on Robert. He passed the 6th grade. He has a new bike thanks to Homer Jones and Bruce Dantzler in Sherwood. He also brought a little friend of his, introduced him as "not as poor as me" but bad off and no bike. So he got a bike. (Robert can con you out of your upper-plate but then he was on the streets of Las Vegas for four years before he came here). We will need food for children this summer and hope with our new van that holds 12 to take some to Magic Springs and maybe to the Zoo. If you have any pull to get tickets to things for children who would otherwise not get to go, send them. Joannie has picked out 10 to take swimming lessons and would not get to go otherwise, and it is taking up two hours of her day for two weeks doing this. It takes another hour to pick them up and deliver them back. Next week she is taking ten to camp for a week. One day at a time we will expose them to the "other side." I was delivering food a couple weeks ago and stopped two little boys and said, "Do you know where so-and-so lives?" They said, "What you doing?" I said, "I am trying to deliver food to poor people. Do you know them?" One of the boys said, "Lady ain't nobody hungrier than us." I took them home, and their parents were outside trying to get a fire started and had a few little fish they had caught. I started unloading some food a restaurant had just given me and they were so happy. I thought they were going to jump up and down. I ended up giving others who lived close the rest of the food.

One of you sent me a check recently, and I took $10 of this money and gave it to a boy who took a bad beating because he protected a small girl who was suffering sexual harassment from (as he said) bad boys when they got off the school bus. I heard about it and rewarded the boy through the school. He did not know who gave the money. I know you will be glad your money went to this brave little poor boy.

Our band performed a concert at the closing of school. They were dressed in their new uniforms and did so well. Thanks for the money some contributed for uniforms. Also thank each of you who helped me buy some band instruments for poor kids who wanted to play but never could afford an instrument. Also thanks for helping me send the whole band by school bus to the Arkansas Symphony. They had never seen anything like that and enjoyed the trip so much. One little poor boy has no bed to sleep on but he has seen and heard the Arkansas Symphony, eaten out and said he would never forget it. (This same little boy helped deliver wood to poor people this past winter in payment for bringing his mother and grandmother a load. He wanted to do this).

The police called me late the other night (I had just gotten in bed from another call). They had picked up a very wet, cold and hungry man from Mexico. The police said he could speak very little English and was so scared. I, at first, told them I could not come up and bring clothes because I would have to go through many bags at midnight at the warehouse to find his size. I said what size does he wear anyway? They said he is a little man about five foot five. I said that is my husband's size. I packed a suitcase with a twenty dollar bill, toothbrush and paste, two sets of underwear, pants, shirts, socks, and a jacket. The next morning they called to thank me and said the man looked so nice (in my husband's clothes) they had decided to try to get him a job and did and wanted me to know. I had prayed things would turn out for him, and I suppose they did.

I took food that had been given me the other day to a house, and the mother was sick, and the child was retarded. The father was helping me get things out of the car. I noticed something growing in the yard. I said, "What have you planted?" He said, "Turnip greens, and I will bring you some and pay you back when they come up." I thought about another poor man I had not thought about in a very long time. He had lost his job because he was unable to do the hard work. I went over to their humble little house and took a box of food someone had left on my porch. I just knew when I saw it where I had to take it. The poor man said, "Mrs. Cayce, I have some English peas I have planted. When they come up, I will bring you some." A while later someone came to my back door. He had brought me a water bucket full of pods of English peas. He said, "These are the first ones I have picked, and I wanted to bring them to you." Here was a man with nothing to give that found a way to "pay me back." I felt as touched as I did when a poor woman came to rake our yard one fall because I had helped her when her house burned.

At the last clothes give-away I was sorting clothes trying to get everything ready, and a poor man came into the Armory. I know pain when I see it, and this man looked like death warmed over. He made it to me and said, "Help me." He started sinking. I held him up and eased him down. He said he thought he had broken his back. He got a man in an old pickup truck to bring him to my house. They told him where I was, and he climbed back in the truck and came another six miles to where I was. I called the ambulance, and they came to the Armory to pick him up. Friends, the poor often have no help or idea what to do. They just suffer.

Please know when you send me a check, we need it and use it for a cause and I often wonder, "What if this check had not come at the time it did?" That alone keeps me so humble and looking up being thankful! I have to stay ready to serve.

A mother came today with two little boys she had just got back from Foster Care. She and her husband have been homeless, and the boys (4 and 7) were taken. They now have jobs and rented a trailer and got the children back. I have kept them fed and clothed, but it has taken them almost a year to get this far. In fact, I got a doctor to see them free a few months ago because they were itching to death from body lice. Being on the streets and sleeping in alleys is tough. I think I wrote you about them. Want you to know they are doing better just needed some food and clothes from me today for

Now I am broke but happy. I know there will be food in kitchens for a week at least, and children will be back in school and getting to eat breakfast and lunch soon. The elderly, of course, are a constant worry. Many had food delivered to them from this give-away who could not get out.

This morning we were going to the Armory with a load of clothes. I was behind the big truck in my van. I saw an old pick-up by the side of the road. I stopped, of course, and saw Pete with his little 8-year-old and another poor, ragged boy. I pulled over and said, "Pete, are you having trouble?" He said, "Yes, Mrs. JoAnn, I ran out of gas. I thought I could make it to town but I ain't able to make it." He said, "I had a pint of gas, in case." I didn't ask him why he was carrying a pint of gas, because I gave up long ago trying to figure out the reasoning of the poor and ignorant. I started to leave, and as I went around, him I saw his radiator was literally spewing water four or five feet from the front of his truck. I pulled over again and said, "Pete, your radiator is busted." He said, "Yes mam, but when it cools off I have a bucket of water in the back of the truck to fill it." I was tickled at his answer, but I did not laugh (I was too close to tears). I said, "Pete, have you got any money to get gas when you get to the station?" He said, "Yes, mam, I got two dollars." He was smiling like he had a pocketful. I told him I had some with me. I got out to help him, and he said proudly, "Miss JoAnn, you knowed I stopped drinking, don't you?" I said, "I heard you had Pete, and I meant to come over and tell you how proud I was of you." (He had a job for the day and didn't get to come to the food give-away, but I sent him a box by his sister). He thanked me for the food sent him and I said, "Pete, has your wife got out of the State Hospital?" He said she had and they gave her some medicine that would help her. I said, "Pete, did you have any money to get the prescription filled?" He said, "Yes mam." That was what he did with the money he earned the day he got to work. I put that down in my book as I drove away (to check on and see about her). Dogs had attack her and torn her arm almost off and dragged her by her leg a long way before someone stopped and ran them off. She also lost an eye in the ordeal and the attack had made her "crazy," Pete told me later. It is a long story and not near over yet. The city said there was nothing that could be done because the dogs got out accidentally. Her doctor bills were not even paid by the owner of the dogs. She is black and poor, and the owner of the dogs is white. I see things like this so often that seem so unfair. Makes me wish I had been a lawyer, but guess if I had been, I might not be out here.

Sherry finally got a place to live with her five children, and now she needs everything. They are on the floor, and she especially needs some mattresses. She has a stove and ice box. We gave her food last Friday but guess it is mostly gone now. She was a battered mother. But I wanted Ms. Joan Anderson (who sent clothes for the new twins) to know they are in a house now. Of course, if they get beds to sleep on they need sheets and cases. Pots and pans and a skillet and dishes would be nice too. I have neglected so many things trying to work on the food give-away and school supplies. It starts Monday, and school supplies and this clothes give-away are a big priority now.

I do thank the Markham Street Baptist Church in Little Rock for the husky clothes for Bobby. I delivered them yesterday, and he will get to start school. Mrs. Crittenden sent panties and socks for his little sister. She also sent some for others. Their mother was killed and your donations helped bury her.

JoAnn Cayce

try to do what I can, and, if it were not for you sending me clothes, money for food and other things, I would be helpless. I will never let you down. A sheriff called me and wanted me to help a man who was getting out of prison this last week, and I put food, clothes, work boots in my swing because I was going to be gone when they brought him down to get the things. I started to walk away and noticed the things and even the $3 I put in an envelope for him had just all been sent or left on my porch in the last couple days. Ms. Hopper, thank you for the money and all the others who leave things. I thank Rita from Pine Bluff who left the bag of food. It went to a family where the man had been hurt on the job, and it will be three or four weeks before he will draw a dime of Workers Comp to keep the family from going hungry. There will be no food stamps or welfare in cases like this because they will draw a check before they have time to qualify for aid. Many times, I stand between hunger and the time it takes to get help (if there is any coming). I thank Charlie Pickle and his friends who came from Illinois to bring all the nice things for our next clothes give-away.

A man came the other day with three beautiful blonde, blue-eyed children and said, "Mrs. Cayce, my children have head lice, and I am off work with an injured knee. I have no water on, no money for head lice treatment, no gas left in my tank, no refrigerator running, and no coats for my children, can you help me? Now out here in rural Arkansas where there is no Salvation Army, no Red Cross, no organization I know of, where would this man go? I called the drugstore and told them to charge me with the lice treatment, and he would be by to get it. I gave him $20 that had come in the mail for gas and for some milk to put on the cereal I had to give him. I later talked to Markham Street Baptist Church about an ice box for them and said I would go get it for the family. I did find coats in your donations for the children and shoes. I gave them food from the food pantry and told him how to get surgery for his knee.

I tell you all these things so you will know these are not just a bunch of deadbeats out here. They are real, live, hurting people with kids and real problems. No, it doesn't get old to me or become more than I can stand. It is not something I get tired listening to. I say this because I am asked that all the time. It never got too much for my mother or my grandmother. I am glad I am here, and it is nothing to brag about or make a big deal out of. They are special to me, and I believe they are special to Jesus. He said, "If you do it unto the least of these, ye had done it unto me." I never reach out that I do not think about this verse.

Sometimes I have to put people off for awhile. The other day a lady came with her son and told me how great their needs were, and her husband was in the hospital and they had no income. I was so busy, so involved with another problem I wanted to tell her to (honestly) "go away." But only for a minute was I tempted. I said, "I will bring you some help and come to your house. Just give me an hour, I will be there." (And I was.) We need food for our Thanksgiving give-away, or money to buy food at 14¢ a pound. This give-away is the 18th of November and Saturday before Thanksgiving, and we need your donations soon. We will have a blanket give-away, pot and pan give-away and a soup give-away, that my grandson Daniel is sponsoring for his Boy Scout badges. If you have anything to help him with this project he will be so thrilled. We won $151 at the fair entering things for prizes, and he has earned money to help himself in his efforts so he is not without merit. We also need coats. We have a man who is 40 inches in the waist who needs underwear and socks. I had pants and shirts for him. I also had soap and towels for him, but he needs a big heavy coat when it gets cold. His work he does is all outside.

For those who have inquired about the dog attack I suffered about two months ago: My bites and torn flesh are all well and the scars are not too bad and for an old woman (68) I have a few battle scars anyway. Ha! The dog did not have rabies. A dog came to our back door yesterday, and I wanted to go out, pet him and help him, but I just shoved out a free meal and said kind words from a crack in the door. Ha.

The elderly will have a nice Thanksgiving with your help, and we will see that they have blankets and hopefully get them plenty of wood for winter for their stove. We have already had men cut some firewood. Deer season is almost here and some bring me deer meat to give to the poor and elderly.

I really have tried to explain to you how these people get into such need because many of you ask and even some consider my causes to be lost causes, and they are not. I promise you there are going to pull up over icy roads to their falling-down house to unload their Christmas. Talk about screaming ... crying ... shouting they were beside themselves! It had taken us 6 hours to unload the 18-wheeler of food and get to the "back" where the other four families and the ----- stuff was. Then to save time, Dr. Suen decided to go in the 18-wheeler down the narrow, ice covered roads to deliver it straight out of the truck. In all my 42 years of playing Santa I never had a sleigh much less an 18-wheeler to deliver folks Christmas. Dr. Suen and family have come a lot of years to help me but never had he had a load like this. I was reeling from having the food given and the 18 wheeler coming to see me, much less having it go to the people's houses over icy country roads. The ----- said their cats could not have lived another day without food. I cried. They did not think of themselves being hungry and cold as much as their animal's sufferings.

One who had been adopted was Robert. I know many of you will be glad to hear Robert has finally landed in a fine home with a nice lady who loves him and is giving him the first home he has ever had. Remember he is the Las Vegas street child who "landed" in Arkansas. He had a wonderful Christmas of food and clothes from the Suens and myself and what some of you sent to him. He got a new bike from Bruce Dantzler and Homer Jones in Little Rock. All in all, it was a wonderful night and when all had left and I sat down for my first meal of the day (about 11:00 p.m.), I laughed and told the family I knew now how Santa felt when he crawled out of his sleigh and pulled his frozen feet out of muddy boots and had his supper.

It is very cold here, there are still hungry families. Late last night we fed a family the leftovers from our own supper, and you would have thought a reheated supper was a feast, the way they went on. We still have folks needing medication and kids needing coats and shoes and we are putting a big clothes give-away together now. We have three loads ready to leave for the Armory in the morning, 2nd. of January, and will reload, unload, and sort as fast as we can. The plans are to have all this out and sorted by the 12th of January at 9:00 a.m. Open the Armory doors and let the pearly gates fly open! You are welcome to come see! Everyone will come in, take all they want free! You made this possible, doesn't that make you feel good?

If you sent boxes of goods, if you sent checks to help me hire help to unload these trucks or buy medication or give out food, pay for heat or wood, get a family help in so many ways, Thank You! Whatever you did to keep us on the road, I mean it, Thank You! I know they say most charities only get 10% to the source but in our case that is not true. I do not take a salary and nothing comes off the top. What you put in our hands gets to the people. I do not have a big desk, a rich carpet in my office, a secretary, or a fancy car. Nothing around here is replaced until it falls apart. I must tell you something right here that I may should have told you 25 years ago. My husband gave me two fine diamond rings many years ago, and my mother left me a big, nice diamond, but I can't wear them! They have been in the lock box at the bank for over 25 years. I cannot wear diamonds into a rat-infested, roach-filled home, where hungry children sleep on the floor. I cannot have a give-away when elderly, crippled, sick and hungry hug me and tell me over and over how thankful they are for the help.

Friends, diamonds lost their attraction for me long ago, and I can't wear them! People in need are more important to me, not diamonds. I had to tell you this. I feel better. I removed the diamonds from my fingers and wear something else in my heart. It is compassion – love! I truly mean this. Thank you for caring about my work. Continue to think of it, please. We need help every day!

Love,

Joannie and JoAnn Cayce

Dear Friend,

Thank you for sending the book, I have not got to read it yet. It takes me longer than used to but I am getting better. Joannie is helping me so much. I hope to get to read it sometime. Excuse this form letter just written to 17 but wanted to send them thanks too for donations for helping me get a load of food.

I have done very little typing since my 3 strokes but wanted to send you a big thank you for all you have continued to do for the poor in this area. I could not have done all I have done if you all had not helped me. I had just had my second stroke Easter, had not gone to the doctor but knew what was wrong. The first one I was out about ten minutes and broke 4 ribs on the right side, this last one, three weeks ago, had to go to Baptist Hospital, and the MRI showed I had had two but the last one did not show up then and would not for awhile. They gave me the medicine that is 70% effective to stop others from following. It is $105 a month, and that, added to my already $525 for heart, diabetes and pressure is rough. Plavix is the name of it. The added dollars plus all the medicine I try to buy for others gets me very depressed, but as I have told others in the past, we are in this for the duration and we will rub noses with Jesus and whisper in His almighty ear and believe tomorrow is going to be better. It hit me last time on the right side and I'm asleep and numb but can move good, which I am so thankful for and realize my great blessing.

I worked long and hard yesterday in getting in food and unloading it. One man and I went after the food at three places, two places are free and one is 14¢ a pound. I picked up clothes at two churches and got home and unloaded. We have done this two days straight. It was hard for me to lift. I then listened to all the messages for the day and culled them some. This morning I started on the "culls" and tried to see which ones were most important. We had a fire at 2 a.m. and got awakened for the night. That is the thing that is hardest being awakened and am not able, no matter how tired, to go back to sleep. I have been told to cut the phone off at 8 p.m., but if a man is beating the crap out of a woman they need me quick. They will not call police. If a baby is bad, I need to get it to the hospital. Since "our kids" insurance, the Governor has made it is much easier on me. Joannie is in the midst of having fundraises and a BarBQ dinner and a beauty contest and a legs (teen age) contest. She is taking a load in a 15-passenger van to Colorado for the World Contest they are hoping to win. They have put their play on from local to state and then National and won all. It is a skit that the poor kids wrote and make all props, costumes and scenes and they dance like you have never seen. They have no lessons and most have never been out of town. This takes $12,000. I just told them I would give what they lacked. They have me as their ace in the hole but if they do not have to use me much they all know they have me at hard times. One man gave $1,000 at the bank and they all had a fit over his gift. Of course he gave for the publicity. I do not need that (publicity) thank God. I got over the ego trips long ago. When God spanks you enough times for thinking "look at me" you soon get over needing a picture in the paper and dinners with big crowds. In fact, there is not time enough for me to attend. I will tell you something funny. I won Blue Cross Person of the Year about two years ago and was so busy, night and day. They wanted me to come accept the award, flowers, be at the luncheon, make a speech. I ask my daughter to go in my place accept everything and tell them it was impossible for me to come. She did and tried to tell something in her speech about her mother when the children were little. They used to go in the old pick-up with me and what fun they would have playing with the poor children with lice and dirt and some with no panties and petting the peoples mangy dogs and giving away their picnic lunch I had packed . She said everyone was in tears and knew everything was real, and she got a standing ovation, and she said she never knew the "poor business" really mattered so much. She had always lived with it, and it was just something we all did, and she took for granted the soup would be gone if they did not get all they wanted at the meal, and that she had to hold the baby if the phone rang and I had to take notes or had to leave quick. I'm really glad I sent her. She said she realized everyone did not have a childhood like she had. She said she never thought too much about all of it when she was growing up. Everyone had a mom who had friends like us and homes like we visited she thought.

My sweet sister went with me one time and she said she would never go again, and it was the saddest day in her life. It was so cold and the old hound dogs were on the floor. There were no beds, and the dogs kept the children who were very sick children from freezing to death. There was no wood for the stove and no food, no lights – that was about ten years ago. Barbara is fighting cancer now and please pray for her. She is 57 and is having to stop her school teaching.

Thanks again for all your help and will appreciate your prayers. They say it will take awhile and I will have to be patient, but I am not too patient about work. It seems I thrive on it. My husband's secretary has left this world, and he has no one but me and Joannie every once in awhile. He is 76 almost and he is out of patience too, ha. He is retired but still does the church papers each month for U.S., stays busy. Thinks the world depends on him to get up mornings. Thanks to your church for their gift also. I am trying to cut corners, so please tell them sincere thanks for all they do for my causes.

Much love,

JoAnn Cayce

Dear Sweet Friend,

I do not know what I would do if those of you who believe in my causes did not help me and trust me and are interested in all that I go through to help any poor human being within about 50 to 60 miles of here. Of course in case someone calls or writes me from farther I try to find them help in their area.

Today in the midst of trying to plan and get up Easter, the Post Master called me and wanted me to go see about a poor soul. She is white and seems to read, write and reason a little bit above what I usually am used to. This lady has not had medication in several months, has diabetes, heart trouble and extremely high blood pressure. When her food stamps did not come in today, she collapsed in tears in the Post Office and told the lady she was hungry and had no medication and was promised food stamps and a Medicaid card would be in the mail. The Post Master called me. I went over, and the lady was living in low condition, her truck was 12 years old and no license, no food, and was ready to trust anyone. I explained myself (wouldn't you like to hear that one?); she grabbed me and started crying and saying she wanted to live for her dogs who were 14, 15 and 16. She had taken them in years ago when someone was going to have them put to sleep because they were old and a bother. I told her I would get her some dog food, her some food and medication. I took her to the doctor and her pressure was 220 over 120 and fasting blood sugar 244. She had lost 22 lbs. The doctor said she was at the stroking stage. She said medication was not had since the first of the year. We got her samples and was told to bring her back Friday. I started trying to figure out in my head how I could do this. Friday was gone, also Thursday, but this was life and death the doctor said. He was amazed she had not had a stroke. This lady is alone and had worked hard all her life. I went for her some food. She needs things I don't have like milk, cheese, eggs, bread and oleo. I will certainly do the best I can but often that is so little because there are so many. This lady is one year younger than I was – 70 this week.

There have been five emergencies this week with others and I have often missed sleep. I fell and hurt my leg this week and failed to have stitches and realize how foolish this was. So sore now to have these, too late. I am doctoring and bathing it. Don't ever do that. I preach seeing doctor and many times doctor diabetics who are foolish to do this. This week it's hard to get time to go to the bathroom.

Joannie has been out of whack. She is working on a play she wrote with poor children doing the acting. I laughed and told her she is trying to teach culture to children who have never heard the word. The play will be presented this coming weekend at a contest at Mountain Home, AR. Everything is so cute. The sun falls and the children, dressed in home made costumes, try to get the sun back up where it belongs. They also try to grow trees where there are no trees, fix housing and teach street people to love and have good days in spite of being poor.

Our program to have help for children with problems getting homework is lots of work and needs more workers and more supplies and refreshments, but it will get off – just takes time. I have my van full of drinks and chips now. If you wish to help that project tell me. There is so much going on that needs your help. Our Easter egg hunt will be the 23rd. Last year there were nearly 350. We hid rabbits, eggs, baskets, toy-filled boxes of whatever we have.

I have been working before day and sometimes before midnight on my will of late. I suppose you have already done this, but it is my pet "put me off" project. My husband will soon be 76, and we both are way behind. We have really had some laughs trying to get our thoughts down on paper so the lawyer can understand our wishes. Since the thief broke into the antique shop and stole so much from us, we have been very sad because he stole our children's inheritance. It takes lots of time to get ready to die, doesn't it. I was working on this the other night and thought "I may not have time to die after all."

I just wanted to tell you about the Easter food give-away for the elderly, sick, families without food, if you want to help. I have canned goods for 900 boxes, but I need something besides canned goods. Dr. Suen from UAMS, and IGA food owners gave me the canned goods, but so much more is needed to make a nice Easter box. I want to do this even if I have to take out a loan, but God always sees us through. Our clothes give-away came out wonderful, and the leftovers were taken to Sparkman, AR., and they had a big give away with our leftovers. We had almost 1,000 here.

My husband gave me beautiful yellow roses, and I have enjoyed the beauty sitting on my kitchen cabinet, but I am thinking about someone who could be with them all day. My sister came to mind. She is home from Baptist Hospital, and her chemo starts this week. She is 12 years younger than me. I had decided to take them to her, but my husband had a fit and ordered her some fresh ones, just like mine. She may not have a breast, but she will have yellow sweet smelling roses and know someone loves her. They will be delivered to her tomorrow. Isn't he truly "Mr. Wonderful?" Thank you for all the packages, checks, thoughts, prayers and encouragement. I hate it that it is all gone, but it went for a good causes and made someone happy,

I love you,

JoAnn, Joannie and Daniel Cayce.

August 1, 2002

I have not mailed everyone a newsletter in some time. I have been ill but have made lots of improvements. It just takes me much longer to do the things I desire to do. For example I used to write a page in ten minutes and now it takes from one hour to two. I have to look up simple words and try to hit the right keys and go over and over to try to correct things. I have had about four strokes they say and three of them happened before I went to the doctor and started medication. This last time I was in Baptist Hospital for a week. They told me I had had a real stroke, not mini stroke or TIA's, and it was of the brain stem this time. That is much harder to get over. I am now walking without my walker but it is slower, and I have to not fall. My memory is not good yet, and I am learning to do many fourth grade things, but I was in first or kindergarten class. I have to have lots of patience. When I am on the phone, which is at least four hours a day, I sometimes cannot think fast. For example yesterday we were trying to get a child with a brain tumor lights and cooling on. They wanted name, SS number and address and how long he had been ill. I used to tell them all that was nuts. He needed lights and cooling now and was terminally ill. He is supposed to have his check start this month. He has to have his mother home to care for him, and she can't work. They just got out of Children's. I finally broke down in tears because it was so frustrating. I would never have done this, before I would have told them off and asked to speak to someone with experience. You may know someone who is fighting to stay alive and learn to live again. Please pray for me, sincerely I need you. I know the danger I am in but I trust in Jesus and as an old poor black lady called to tell me a few weeks ago. She said, "Mrs. JoAnn, just put your hand in Jesus' every day and say 'By your stripes I am healed.'" My poor people are afraid too. I hate this so much. They have enough trouble.

The food bank is next door, and Daniel and my other grandson bagged cereal last week and we also took 48 elderly and poor food in boxes. They were people without who had no transportation. They were so glad to see me. I also helped to clean out the warehouse and we got a load of toilet tissue in and gave much out. We are giving out Little Debbies, cake mix, hamburger helper, crackers and cereal this next week when poor people come to pay their water bills at the City Hall. A little help is better than none, and we have enough for about 500 and don't want it to go to waste.

I wanted to tell you I got a doctor to see the homeless, 33-year-old lady who has blood pressure of 300 over 120. The doctor who saw her free and gave her samples has died and she has not had medication since Dec. If I buy medication, this doctor will see her free after first visit which I paid for. This lady is so very pitiful, but we are doing the best we can. Of course you know this summer and children need food and fathers have been laid off from jobs or mothers have to stay home with school children. Some make so little they can't afford to hire children sitters.

Joannie and Daniel are like lifesavers. Since I can't drive right now, they help in everything. I feel like the most blessed person in the world.

We want to thank you for the donations sent. I know many think I am ill and we do not need money, but nothing could be farther from the truth. We actually need more because lots of things they cannot do, and I have to hire a man to help, but we do not hire anyone unless we have to. My other grandson from Georgia who stayed with us two weeks, left here needing a vacation from his vacation, but he seemed so proud of being able to help. He is 15, and I wish he lived closer. Daniel's friends sometimes help. We are trying to get Daniel a hardship license so he can drive to the warehouse and drive me to see about people.

If anyone has any kind of band instrument for children and teenagers to please let children who can't afford an instrument have a chance to make music. Band has started, and the instruments you gave me last year are still in use but we need more. I am not serving on the school board this year, but Joannie is running and she is so much in hopes you will look in your attic or under your bed and have a heart for these children who have nothing unless you care. We will get them right to the band room at Bearden High School.

I wanted you all to know I am closing out my antique shop I have operated on weekends for nearly 40 years. I am now 70 and I want to not have to worry about the time it takes from my poor people. Joannie and I are starting to write my book, and I can do this while I am not working. Also since the thief took so much from me, I just lost interest. I also feel he stole my health. I had my first stroke when the first robbery happened, and I fell and broke my right ribs. If they had taken MRI of my head instead of my ribs, they would have seen what really happened, and I could have started on the blood thinner. This world is full of ifs. I am not the only one who would like to go back. Please help me in begging for more time to serve.

I just wanted you to know things are still going on as much as ever but harder. Please continue to pray. I know the danger I am in and how far I have come, and how far I still need to go. I am so thankful for yesterday and don't want to forget to be thankful for every blessing.

Love you so much,

JoAnn Cayce

Dear Friends,

Today we started moving the used toys to the Gym where we will give them away to little poor children for Christmas. We have done this for over 35 years. Seemed we had more names this year and less used toys. Part of my "blueness" was, of course, my tired body of 71 years had taken so many hits this year. I have had four strokes, a broken leg, broken ribs, heart surgery and terrible time with asthma and a battle with my diabetes.

But as I worked alone with a very tall, very poor black man of 40, whom I had known since he was born, I began talking to him about his childhood. What started it was I found in the donations a stick horse in good shape, and I thought it would make some little child very happy. I said, "Benny, I bet you would have loved to have had one of these when you were a child, wouldn't you?" He looked it over and tears may have been only my imagination, but he said "Mrs. Cayce, I never had a toy when I was a child except one I made."

He said, "I made me a little car, and one time I made me a whistle." I asked him what his Christmas was like in those days. I said, "That was before I started seeing that all children I knew had one thing at Christmas." He started talking, and I started crying and all my "blueness" over our small supply ended and I became very sorry I even wished for tons of new toys. He said there were 8 of them and they lived in four rooms and his father started drinking on Friday with all he made working in the woods that week if he got to work.

The house leaked all over and was freezing cold and wet in the winter. They tried to move the places they had to sleep out of the cold, wet rain. He said they were hungry all the time and never had a coat or sweater. He was big as a child, and he could never get clothes to fit him and shoes always hurt if he had a pair. He wears size 20 now, and I get people to send him shoes that live close to factories that sell that size. I try to keep him in a coat which he needs replacing badly. He said he never had a pair of gloves until I bought him the pairs I have given him through the years. Once I went over to take a picture of his almost 8 foot frame for Social Security, and before I snapped the cheap picture I remember him asking, "Mrs. Cayce, will it hurt?" I feel sure he has never had ice cream, a good steak, a pair of warm pajamas or even a comfortable mattress, to name a few of the finer things of life. I doubt he ever will or even dreams of the possibility.

He said he never had a Christmas gift, and he used to lie awake listening to his mother try to talk his drunken father into letting her have a few dollars before he drank it all up. He said he knew his father would beat them up to "get back" at her for spending a dime on them. He said he would rather have a bowl of gravy and some bought loaf bread. He said his father, every Christmas all his life, would start a fight with his mother on Thursday night and use that as an excuse for not giving her any money to spend.

He said as he laid in the room with all his brothers, he would want to scream "hush," but he didn't dare. He doesn't read or write today and never did. He didn't play basket ball in spite of his giant height, he did not get to go to school. He swept leaves, killed hogs, and did a million chores from the age of 5 or 6 and never got to keep a dime. He gave it all to his mother if his father did not take it before he gave it to her. I asked if that made him mad, and he said, "It still do," and his father died in the early 80s. No one had paid any attention or showed him any affection all his life, and he is so quiet, shy, and withdrawn I was completely surprised he talked to me about things he must have kept all his life. Benny has gaintism, and will not live long. He mostly has lived his life now according to records, but neither he nor his people know this. I worry if I should tell them, or would any one care?

When he was young someone gave him a banana, and he dreamed for years how it tasted. I asked him if he ever had an orange, pineapple, or apple, and he said he never saw one until he was a "great big kid and I started getting food give to me to give away," and he saw and tasted things he never had before.

Now for all the young people over this country who read this and complain about what is under the tree this year "Shame"…be glad and thankful and remember the 7'8", 40-year-old man who never had a radio much less a television in his life and has to duck to get in a shack that none of you would keep your precious pet in and thinks a picture would "hurt" if he let someone take a picture and who has been beaten, whipped and cursed all his life – who has never been able to get a driver's license or go to "town" to see the Christmas lights or even had a Christmas tree at home, who has never had a Christmas or Thanksgiving turkey for that matter. I doubt that he even knows there is such a thing as an electric blanket or a computer. It is a shame that the young people of today want a certain brand, a certain kind of tennis shoe, when this boy would give his life for a pair of shoes that didn't hurt and a warm coat – a boy who has never had your families love, security, peace, joy, or even the presence of a Mom and Pop who love each other and respect family and all it means. Be thankful and look at the other side of the coin, but for the grace of God, there goes ye.

JoAnn Cayce

November or December 2002

Dearest Friend,

The Thanksgiving give-away is past (yesterday), and we are trying to get over the loss of energy and the tiredness. Joannie and Daniel and I are all just elated over the things we saw and felt and the things that took place. Channel 11 was here and covered it. I did not get to talk with them. I think others did and it will be aired on Monday at 5 and on Tues morning at the news.

We got Popsicles from Brenda at Warren, for 20 dollars about 400 boxes with about 100 in each box, and they had to be frozen.

They were just unfrozen juice, and we gave them out a box at the time. Joannie thought I should not have spent money we did not have, but I just had a feeling I should. We also bought all the sets of dishes for $2 each she had for the people who had never had a set of dishes. They were seconds. We thought if we ran out of blankets we would give a set of dishes, we did run out of blankets. We had over 1,600 and started on dishes, and they all were so thrilled they forgot the cold without blankets.

A man had given us 290 gallons of milk. We had no cold space and I thought we would have to give it out when we had no time that night. But Joannie made an "ice box" out of a huge wood box that was 6'by 6', would hold it all, and she covered top and bottom with heavy quilts and insulation and we put some frozen things included. Two days later it was still freezing cold in the box, and we started giving it out of course at the give-away Saturday. Daniel had about 900 and I had less than that, but by not much. He gave out every thing he had which was apples, milk, blankets, dishes, popsicles, all medicine, bread, rolls as the people called them the sweet rolls, etc. The people went wild over the bologna and the bread – they actually cried. But the story I wanted to tell was the little boy no older than 8 who slipped in the side door, and I was standing there. I started to tell the very, very ragged, thin child he had to go around, that this side was the side to go out. I could not do it. I do not know how he knew I was "boss," but he looked at me so sad and said, "Could I have a box of Popsicles?" I did not ask him if he had gotten his groceries or his mother because I thought his mother might not have come, and he said he caught a ride from home. I went to get his popsicles, and he asked, when I came back to him, if he could get some of "them apples." I said yes and as I walked away he called, "Could I have a jug of that milk?" I came back and looked again to see if his little arms were as thin as I had first thought, and they were. He grabbed the things and I was about to ask him where he lived and who he was because there are few children I do not know. He had all this stuff in his little arms, and everyone was going out hitting me and him and he said to me, "Could I have another jug of milk for my little brother and sister – they ain't got none?" I wanted to say no, but there stood this 8-year-old about half the size he should be and who was for sure scared to death. I said, "You can't carry another jug of milk." He put his bag of apples in his rotten teeth and said, "Yes I can." I went after a jug of milk and came back and he managed to get the milk in his little thin arms. He started leaving in a hurry, and I realized I did not know his name. This was probably the only milk he had had in years. I was so glad we had milk. Every scrap of milk, bread, bologna, blankets, fries, sweets, we got in so late the night before and the patent medicine and rub was given away, and one old fellow maybe 85 told me he was so happy to get his cold medicine. He had Vicks and nose drops and several other things we had. I said, "Did you get your blanket?" He said he got his milk and medication and his box of groceries, and he would have a wonderful Thanksgiving. He was so pitiful and weighed maybe 100 lbs. I thank all who helped us buy food and those who gave food. We never use or waste stuff and if the ones who gave the bread were here I would hug them. The stuff was worth staying up all night for because the 18 wheeler did not get in until 11 p.m.. Joannie and Daniel and I worked and got it put in all boxes we had fixed for two weeks before and also the pizza dough – I know they had never had that. One woman said she was going to eat it with her greens. They did not know it was pizza, in fact, I doubt if they had ever had pizza. It was wonderful, and with my limited energy this morning, I had to tell you wonderful people who helped or prayed how this went over. I hope you feel like helping us with toys for Christmas or a few dollars for toys, clothes, or candy and fruit for the holidays. We also got $345 in money to help with toys for children, and Daniel got $20 to help on his next project. He is thinking he would like to get more Popsicles to put in every child's Christmas bag at Christmas but that is a 15-year-old thinking. If we could get someone to give bags for children's toys, etc. – we have so little money. We need the leaf size bags about 600 for very needy children, and they could use them later for trash and getting jobs raking during the holidays. If you have a used child's warm coat we sure need them. We could never thank everyone who helped. We especially thank the Little Rock Oak Park and Markham Street Churches who sent buses to help wait on the people and Channel 11 and all the encouragement they gave us. It is so joyful to see the joy in people's faces who give time and who help us.

Happy Holidays,
JoAnn, Joannie, and Daniel Cayce.

If you want to help Christmas, do. We are just trusting like from day to day. We will give out bags on Dec. 20.

God Opened a Flood (of good)

Christmas has just passed, and 2003 has arrived. We hope and pray you had a great holiday and will have the best and healthiest year of your life in 2003. You have done much for us during all the years past, but in 2002 I think you have supported us with more prayers and more patience than we have ever experienced. Some weeks we could not have survived without believing in the answer to prayer (yours and ours). Different people have remarked to me and to Hartsel that we have had the most trying year they have ever heard of. These are people who have not remembered Job or have not known many families we know. It has been rough, I admit that, but I know in many ways it could have been so much worse. Now for a happier note, let me tell you about some miracles that have just taken place here in our home, town, and surrounding areas.

All year Joannie, Daniel and I had saved new clothes, toys, coats, cosmetics, and bikes for poor children's Christmas at a warehouse, waiting for Christmas. On Monday December the 9th, two men and I started moving these things to the gym, where we were going to sort and make trash bags filled with Christmas for about 600 children. Names were coming in since December first of children who would have no Christmas. Children are referred to us by Head Starts, schools, DHS, churches, CADC, men who read water meters, police, jails, and families. This is the way poor children with no Christmas (or much of anything else) are found. We have depended on the Marines to help us with their Toys for Tots program every year, for many years. We thought we could not do with out them. We underestimated the working of the Lord. He does care about poor children who are handling the situation, but He had not started the BIG flood yet. I went to the doctor to see about my leg on the 18th of December, and we came home to a bedroom literally filled with packages and large envelopes. To date, we have received not only socks but panties, boys underwear, caps, gloves, scarves, sweaters, cosmetics, combs, brushes, toothpaste, brushes, barrettes, house shoes, gowns, PJs, and many small items I can't remember. Children got hands full of these in every bag. Joannie said she had never expected anything like this. She said God may have allowed my leg to be broken, but He gave me something useful to do instead of sitting crying and worrying. Every child was taken care of through December 28, and the packages are still coming in. In fact, today is the 2nd of Jan., and Hartsel just brought in mail sacks and dumped them by my wheelchair. Don't ever doubt God, folks. He takes care of His poor. That song "Does Jesus Care" has an answer.

Besides all the packages, a man from New York came who read the website and brought a large Ryder truck filled with fruit and groceries, clothes and toys. Joannie and Kandy, who was home for the Holidays, helped him deliver it to needy homes all day Monday before Christmas. There was also an 18-wheeler sent filled with food on Saturday, and it seemed impossible to get it unloaded since Joannie was giving out Christmas. But little did I know she had a gym full of volunteers, and they all came and formed a line and got it off the truck quickly. Two men from Chicago came with a load on Sunday morning and had driven until 3 a.m. that morning and had to get unloaded and return to Chicago to go to work Monday. Daniel and Kandy's husband, Ted, helped them unload and they stayed awhile and helped Joannie give out emergencies on our front porch. They were so touched to see and do. Another man has promised to come with a load of mattresses and home needs in January for that give-away. So many sleep on the floor and one grandmother called and wanted a mattress for her grandchild whose springs were coming out of the mattress she slept on.

To date, we have received about 500 tubes of tooth paste, over 20,000 pairs of socks and a ton of odds and ends. Our food pantry is stocked for weeks now. We have coats and some blankets. WHO CAN COMPLIAIN ABOUT A BROKEN LEG???????

Dear Precious People,

I have wanted to write a general charity letter for almost a year but seemed there just was not enough time. I know you wanted the news and how things were going, and this is the news and hopefully it won't be so long next time. I have tried to write the ones who sent some help and thank them. But for those who were not able I guess this is the first time you have heard in some time. Not because we do not love you but for the reason given we did not write you. But keep in mind we think about you and always want to hear from you and your family. Things still continue as much as finances allow.

We give food to families every day. We fed 11 families yesterday. Channel 4 came the day before and took pictures of our food bank and Daniel's school supplies, his school back pack program and the county judge giving an award to him for his service to the elderly and the thousands of jars of baby food he has given to tiny babies who have no WIC to cover baby food and no parents who can buy it. He works each evening and weekends in some sort of program, and sometimes his friends help him.

We had our tremendous Easter Egg Hunt on Good Friday, and we had 900 kids and some parents. We fed them till they nearly popped. Daniel got a company to give him ice cream and popsicles, and we (Joannie and I) furnished (with some of you to help) cookies, punch, muffins, chips and candy. It was a bright sunny day and we hid 2,000 eggs with the help of others who stuffed eggs and mailed them or brought them. I was so thrilled to see the children run across five acres gathering eggs, candy, stuffed toys, rabbits and chickens. It was covered by Channel 4 also and if you did not see it watch June 25 at 7 p.m., the awards night when they will give Daniel the Teen Humanitarian Award for the State of Arkansas and show all the pictures they took. Most of these children will have no other Easter except the one we provide, and we put extra effort in making them happy. We gave many of your dresses, pants, jeans and shirts to dress these kids, and they looked so nice. It did the parents good to have a day out with the children, and they enjoyed the food and fun also. We gave away hundreds of Easter Baskets thanks to Mitz Mosier and ladies who work at the Behavior Clinic in Sherwood, AR. They spent weeks getting many things ready. Right now the most pressing thing is getting a very thin, poor mother-of-three children's teeth pulled and anything you want to send, send to Dr. Kaufman DDS 305 Graham Street, Fordyce, AR 71742 who started pulling them last week or send to us for Brenda's teeth. We are trusting by the time they are all pulled to be able to get her false teeth to replace her rotten ones. Dr. Kaufman will also do the false teeth ask him to credit Brenda that JoAnn is helping get false teeth. He is doing them at a price that is not cheap, but he will let me pay them out. Some of you may remember she is the lady who was at the give-away who was so very thin and had a mouth filled with rotten teeth off to the gums who kept her hand over her mouth. She is now the happiest lady I have worked with in a long time. I think she was down to 70 pounds and so unhealthy because she could not eat. She is now living on Daniel's baby food. Her living conditions would break your heart, but we are hoping we can stick with her and see this through. The last one I had their teeth pulled, I had to let heal for several months and saved money and before we could start on the false ones she called me and said "Mrs. Cayce, when you goin' bring me my store-bought teeth?" It never occurred to me she thought I could go to Wal-Mart and get her some new teeth. I'm amazed everyday at the ignorance I face. I weep for the pain some endure before I find them or they find Joannie or me. The man who came and took pictures with me taking him around cried over what he saw, and I told him that was the hardest part was seeing. I work and pray and so does Joannie that Daniel never will get used to telling his buddies "There is no time for tears out here, guys, you just got to work".

Remember Benny at Christmas who lives with his 90 year old mother? Well their commode stopped working and they are going to the woods behind their house. I promised him to fix it this week and let him work it out. I have never had anyone work out a toilet before. I will, of course, have to pay up front and then Benny will work out the debt. He tried to fix it himself before he came to me and I hope did not make it worse. Thank the ones who sent him jeans and shoes. The shoes were too small. He is almost 8 foot and wears a size 20 wide shoes. He won't live much longer but is the one who had never had a Christmas gift. Anything sent him you must say for BENNY. I will get it right to him. He is very deserving.

We had a mother come who wanted a bed, so if anyone of you have an odd bed or mattress, we could give away a 100 before dark. So many sleep on the floor. Take it to Markham Street Baptist Church in Little Rock, and tell them you want to put it in JoAnn Cayce's room or take it to Kandy's, our daughter's carport in Sherwood. Their Number is 835-3013. We go almost every week also Mr. Homer Jones at 3000 Seminole Trail has a garage and he will keep it for us and call us. I need all kinds of furniture, no matter the condition.

I know you think everyone has as much as they need but this is farther from the truth than you can guess. This was brought home to me when a mother told me she wanted all the stubs of pencils for her children and chips of soap to melt. I finally found out her children needed tiny short pencils that alot of people throw away. We are out of cereal now and need some badly. We have 1,000 pounds of dry milk, but the cereal source dried up. I can't remember being out of cereal before, but Kellogg is selling it to General Dollar Stores now. I know we would give them what they are getting, but hard to make them believe it. I am nobody.

I have gotten so many emergency calls this morning it is hard not to get blue or stop trying to find solutions. One boy had a bad infection and needed antibiotics. The doctor did not work with me, and I told him it had to be penicillin because that was cheap. He wanted me to explain why I thought I was smarter than him about choosing the medication. I tried to tell him what I did, and that a $90 one was not one I could afford. He laughed. It is hard to tell anyone I am paying for medication, and that I have to have it cheap because there are so many needing help. This gives me the right to ask for something I can pay for. Penicillin is so cheap. I can get 44 pills for a little less than $3. He is not allergic to them, and I think he should prescribe something he or I can buy. He got hurt cutting wood for the kitchen stove. Another man came whose jaw was so swelled, and he was in such pain he was crying. He said a Dr. Brown said he needed to have four abscessed teeth pulled at once. Our barn needs the tin nailed on it. I asked him if he would fix it when he got better, and he fearfully agreed. Think if he is willing to work I can trust him to pay the bill with work. I paid for his teeth so that charity bill is paid. It takes someone keeping records on bills that I have coming and what the charity has coming. I sure want to keep it straight. We got the charity storage fixed this week by another out-of-work man who needed food for his wife and children.

As most of you know I am closing, or have closed already, the Antique Shop by the house after 35 years. It is hard not to have money especially when emergencies come. I am trusting the Lord to see that no one goes hungry. Joannie is finished with her chemo and her hair is about two inches long and she looks good without the wig she has worn for four months now. I am up and walking after the strokes, and both of us together make one woman pretty able to work, and Daniel is a bonus. Joannie cooked 150 hamburgers for a project they had going this week. I told them I would be their cashier, but they were too afraid I would fall. They do all manner of things to raise money. They had a Barbecue supper this last week, and this is for kids to go to Washington DC. I never did do any of this. I used to go to churches to let me have a bus or Greyhound to take a load to the zoo or McDonalds to feed a hundred or so kids that had never been to McDonald's, but I never did try to raise money like they do. I just cooked for people on Thanksgiving and Christmas and 4th of July. It got where this was too much, and I had to stop. I started the food give-aways then, and this proved very successful and would feed people for a week. We got kids to help and Daniel's friends. I really think young people want to feel needed. They seem to be willing to help Daniel, and Daniel told me the girls ask him when we will have another promotion. He won a speaking contest at Arkadelphia and will now enter the contest a UAMS. He is doing this for college help, so I admire him for this. He said he just speaks from the heart. One college dean called the Bearden High School and said he just happened to sit in on a contest at his college, and he was so touched by Daniel's speech he wanted to call and tell the superintendent. I was so proud. I have not had anymore strokes in a year or more so am very encouraged. Pray for Joannie. I depend on her and Daniel to carry this poor business on.

This morning I took an elderly lady some meat who has a very hard time on her small check, and she told me they had cut her food stamps again and her medicine bill was so high she was having to choose between food and medication. She is living on rice and beans and macaroni. I promised food once a week. I know a man who will be glad to take her a dozen eggs a week from his chickens, and that will make a difference. This is a lady who worked hard all her life, and I don't know how she could have done differently. Her husband died before I got grown, and she never remarried. She is uneducated but very hard working before she got on a walker. When you see it, folks, it makes it real. These are real people and a little bit of food or help makes a difference you can feel.

If you fuss about the old lady's yard needing mowing, is she able? Does she have the money to hire it? Don't forget us. If you have anything that can be used or left over like a pair of glasses, samples of anything from motels or hotels or small bits of soap mail it to 415 South Second or Box 38, take it to the church or Kandy in Little Rock. You do not have to be rich, but you just have to be unselfish and think of others. Of course I can always use a few dollars and work very cheap (nothing). I just want to feel it where it matters and give back. Any company you think might help us with tooth brushes and paste, tell them about us.

I Love you,

JoAnn Cayce

Dear Friends,

Today it is raining and cold, and Joannie has gone to Little Rock to get food from the Rice Depot, but they have no canned food or meat. She will get what they will let her have, and we will, as my mother used to say, make do.

We had the Thanksgiving give-away last Saturday the 20th of Nov., and there were about 3,000 there. All races and all ages. We gave everything we had.

We saw people without jobs begging for a second box. We saw one lady who had nothing she could eat because she is having her teeth pulled and begging for soup and liquids. A little boy came up to me and said, "My mother is getting a box, blankets and coats, but I am so hungry now. Could I have something out of a box – anything?" One of the volunteers from Oak Park Church in Little Rock (they sent a bus load of folks to help) told me he would take care of the child. Soon a blonde-headed lady came down the line and she wanted to tell me her troubles, but I told her she must come to our house or call – the line had to keep moving before it rained on the 100s waiting under dark clouds. Besides being hungry and no Thanksgiving, the crowd all had troubles like you have never heard. I thought the only thing these folks have NOT to worry about that you might is Identity Theft. No one wants their identity. It was a sad and tiring day but a happy one because so many were smiling and hugging me and happy about the food. Daniel gave out of blankets, and he gave out about three fourths of the way through and was very heart sick he could not wait on all those who came cold and without. He had his give-away on one side of the gym and we were on the other. He had personal items and soap, baby food, school supplies and blankets of course.

Just before the give-away, Bob Mack in Little Rock, got a huge supply of instant potatoes and we added them to the 1,000 boxes, and this was a big lift. We had a huge supply of coats, sweaters and warm sweat pants. They went through these till in the afternoon. Only one box of food to the family but Daniel gave out blankets to lots of children who said they slept cold.

Now we are facing Christmas. There are already more names than last year and we will not start taking names till next week on the first of Dec. We have dolls, Joannie fixed. Daniel and Joannie have our sun porch filled with dolls that have all been bathed and shined in the past three or four weeks. We collected Barbie's too, and she bathed and put them in new clothes and new hairdos, so we do not have to worry about dolls. We need about 400 basketballs for sure, more tooth paste and brushes, underwear , socks, sweaters of all sizes, tennis shoes of all sizes and anything for teenage girls, old makeup, perfumes bath powder, costume jewelry.

We have a family who has moved to town at a very bad time, when we are pushed to the limit, but the father abandoned them, and they came here because they heard about us. The mother has 11 children. Now, if you think that won't keep you awake at night, you are wrong. They need everything, especially food. We have temporarily taken care of that and got them all in school and Daniel put them on his after-school feeding program and weekend back-pack program. In five more weeks they can get food stamps.

One little girl came with neighbors to the food give-away this weekend and she was looking through some clothes long after most everyone was gone. I went up to the lady she came with (I thought she belonged to) and said, "How many coats are you looking for and what sizes and I will help you." I turned to the ragged little children and pointed to the little child about 10 and said, "What size do you think she will wear?" The lady said, "Oh, she don't belong to me, she just came along. She is looking for her own stuff." I looked at the little blonde-headed child with dirty body, hair stringing down, and I never wanted a child to go home with me more. She was so tiny and big sad eyes. She needed a hair cut, shampoo and shoes. She had on flip flops, and it was so cold. I put my arm around her, feeling her skinny shoulders and said, "Sweetheart, let's get you a coat." She pulled back and said, "I just found this coat." The lady said, "Oh, she done got a coat, that is it she's wearing and wants to wear it home." I looked at it, and, worn as it was, it was new and warm to her. Who ever mailed the brown coat about size 8 with the fake fur for a little girl, it has a good home, not too clean but it is loved.

We went to Washington D.C. with Joannie and Daniel and I did fine. I was stronger climbing and walking than I thought. Daniel had to make speeches in three different places and he only thought he would have to say "thank you" when he got his award. He made it fine, and this was a big to-do, more than we thought. The dinner was out of this world. There was so much sliver we needed sun glasses. I was so impressed at all the fanfare. They had come up with the Hall of Flame awards since I won one in '92. There was no food then and no breakfast brunch we were invited to. A big tour bus took us everywhere, and we had lunch at the Union Station. There was so much food left one day I had to ask the host if it were being tossed, and they looked at me funny and I told them I would be glad to get a taxi and hand it out to the homeless we saw on the street outside. They told me it would go to a shelter, and I hope this was true – would be a shame if eggs and all the fruit and potatoes and raw vegetables were tossed. Daniel was doing great things on a small budget, and the other four kids were impressive, but none worked with the poor. One collected house shoes for a hospital, one tried to promote No Smoking, one gave away kids' books to hospitals, one was in memorial by her parents when she got killed in car wreck and they set up a foundation for kids to go to college. The people were so touched by what Daniel did. He got a college check for $2,000 and all expenses for all of us. He is so proud of that.

Daniel was invited by actors Ted Danson and Mary Steenburgen to the Clinton Library opening, and he made a speech there. They were so kind to him, and Senator David Pryor said some nice things about him and me. I have known him and his family for years, but Daniel had never met him.

Something good for the people might come of all this and Daniel missing a day of school. Really, Daniel is sort of like me – big to-dos do not impress him or me. We had rather be working but this was great and we were treated like kings.

I wanted all of you who helped us to consider this a special thank you for the help mailed us and the packages sent. All these things keep us going. We got food as your checks came in from the sources and tried to make the give-away better, and this all was spent for the good of children and families. Someone gave us three dozen eggs today, so no gift is too small. A lady gave us a turkey yesterday, and when Joannie got home from getting it, I asked her about it, and she said, "I have already given it to a large family who had none." She never got home with it. Our list is long and sad, and there is no question about who needs what. Sometimes God impresses us before we have time to think about who.

Daniel often gets discouraged (like Saturday when he ran out of blankets and baby food), but I told him we might not be able to feed the world, but we keep many children warm and will never stop trying. If you send any of the above items please write on outside of box "CHRISTMAS." We might get to open just clothes or regular things till after the holidays. Remember the late stuff helps us take care of emergencies . Above all, pray for us and our energy. If you are touched to send a few dollars we will be ever grateful. Our needs are great this time of year. We love you and thank you so much.

Love,

JoAnn, Joannie and Daniel

Dear Sweet Friend,

I first want to tell you the big give-away will be (Lord willing) next Saturday, Aug. the 21st. It has taken weeks to get this ready. We have been giving out food and helping people all this time but it is with great difficulty.

I have had more things happen to me lately than I can grasp.

I have come to the edge (of life), and God pulled me up by a thread the doctors said. The specialist said, to me, himself, to give the Man above the credit and not him. He said, himself, he wanted no credit for the miracle I had.

I had fallen out cold several times and was so dizzy all the time I could hardly walk. My head was so loud I could hardly hear and my right eye was almost out.

My heart doctor decided I might have blocked arteries to the brain. I was blocked to my brain 70 to 80 %(they found it was blocked 95% later). The blood supply to the brain was almost shut off. They wanted to do more tests to see if I could be saved. I went to the hospital and had a dye test of my arteries. The only doctor who did this Neuro-Radiology surgery in Arkansas was at a meeting and could not get back till the next week.

A man in the lab told me this week, when I had had the operation and got along so well, the lab people knew the specialist was gone who might could help me and there was no one else there who could do this surgery. He said none of the people in the lab thought I would live to Monday to get back up there, when the doctor got back. God saw to it I lived until the next week. That "thread" they said I was holding onto, held like steel. I came home went about my business. I went to church, but was careful.

I was told the next week I had no chance without the surgery. I was told I may have a massive stroke on the table but it would only be a matter of time (short) until I would have a massive stroke, so I had to take the chance. Word went out, people started praying.

An old black woman who was so poor and many of you have paid for food for her and her little children all these years. I had known her all my life, and my mother had helped her get a home for her children when her husband was killed working in the woods. When my mother died nearly twenty years ago I started tending to her business and helping her feed her children. She paid off her home over the years and her children grew up and left home. She is the prayingest lady I know. Through the years she has helped me pray for Joannie and hundreds of things. Before Daniel was born when times were so tough, I would go up in the "alley" where she lived, and we would pray for his safe birth. She heard about this last problem and walked to our house. She does not read or write and has nothing of the worlds goods. She came to the door and I opened it, and she grabbed me and loved and kissed me over and over. I explained everything to her as best as I could. She continually cried. She begged to go to hospital with me the next morning at 4 a.m. August 10th I told her Joannie and Hartsel would take me, and it was almost a hundred miles, and I had no way of getting her back. I told her I would be in intensive care and could not care for her. She begged and said "I will sat in ther' with you." It was so hard, seeing her suffer. I finally convinced her it would be more help for me for her to stay home and pray. The next morning a crowd came to the hospital, and there was much praying Paul Cayce, told me later.

So now I am home recovering and looking forward to next Saturday and as many more Saturdays as the Lord will grant me in response to all those prayers, for which I will be eternally grateful.

With love,

JoAnn Cayce

Dear Precious Friends, (It is New Year's Day)

There are about 41 of you who have helped us so much and some of you have also sent us a beautiful card during this season of the year. We have received from 555 cards to about 700. I did not keep count toward the last. Thank you who enclosed checks and $1 up plus a goat for the hungry people to raise it to and have milk and a herd later. We have gotten help in many forms but never in the form of a goat. Thanks for everything – cards, checks, cash, and yes, a goat. I used to not think of a card as something until I had no time to send them at all, and I went in the drugstore one day and Mrs. Ross was crying and I asked her what was wrong. She was the pharmacist's wife. They were like me in those days, no time. She said, "Well, did you see that ragged boy who just went out?" I said, "Yes." She said, "Well, he has a mother who can't get out of bed and is dying. He just handed me this card and said they could not send but one card and since me and Ross had been so good to keep his mother in medication between her check-ups they had decided to give us the card, but they did not have money to get a stamp, so he walked to town to bring it to us." After that I thought of all the poor people who sent us cards as well as the people who have money, and I thought I will take the time to love cards and I have. I hope you will excuse this way of sending you a letter for the holidays. We love you and thank you for remembering us.

We are so far behind and are trying to get a clothes and coat and shoes give-away. We also have tons of all types of clothing. We are upset because we have lost the gym until the basketball season is over in Feb. The folks need clothes right now, but it takes 1 month to get all sorted and out on the full width and length of the gym, and they need that to play.

So much happened this Christmas that it is hard to describe. I think since this is on my mind I will tell you this first. There was a family moved into town, close to my brother, and he talked to me about the sadness of the situation – so cold and no heat and they had no way to get supplies or deposit for heat. He said they had no food, jobs, coats, the house was a shack that the man let them move in to fix up fit to live in (that will take a miracle). They did not have plastic to put over the windows where the panes were gone. How he came to go over and "make friends," he saw the little 8-year-old boy with no coat, playing out in cold and building a fire outside. His dog had strayed, and he went over to see if the child had a coat and if he would watch out for his dog. He said the child asked if he had a cookie or candy. My brother said the sight was so sad. He asked the child where his mother and dad and the little girl he had seen over there were. He said they were looking for a little work and a job and the sister was asleep. He said they had moved in with nothing, and it was 17 degrees. He said he started trying to help them, and would I see that the children had some Christmas and a coat and some food. I told him I would get down there with emergencies quick. I was so very busy and expecting a load of people to come in who were staying with us and the beds were not made upstairs from the ones who just left. I dropped everything and gathered coats, food, plastic, blankets, and planned Christmas for a 10-year-old girl, 8-year-old boy and a mother who had an abscessed tooth and a father without a job. I went down there in the afternoon, and the mother had gotten work but was hurting so bad and swelled it was pitiful. I left everything and went back to call a dentist. He said he would see her free. I went back, and my brother was working on the heat. The man was working with him and had a few days work starting the next day. Got her to dentist and had the tooth pulled and all the food was so much appreciated. I went the next day to check on the mother, and the daddy was gone to work and there was an "odd boy" there about 8 or 9. I asked him why they were not in house because of the cold. My brother had gotten on the heat in one room and a heater (he had paid the deposit). It was seven days till Christmas. I asked the "odd" child who he was, and he looked at the 8-year-old who lived there and said he lived in Camden, a town close. I said, "Are you kin to him?" he looked so ragged, scared, needed a hair cut and so thin. He said, "I am his almost cousin." I looked at the stay-there child and said, "He said he was your 'almost cousin.' What does that mean?" The stay-there blue-eyed blonde child said, "He is my almost cousin and when my momma and daddy get married he will be my 'sure enough cousin'" (any fool should understand that). We gave Christmas to over 800 children plus old people in nursing home and hospitals. Daniel went back to the nursing home and went to see the two men who had nothing or anyone to see about them. We didn't go with him as the house was full and so much to do, but he chose to go alone. He said it was so sad to see someone with no love in their life and he had so much. We saw family after family come to get Christmas and bring the children. It was the most Christmas they would see. Many did not have a tree and many had seen no Christmas lights. I give them what I can and do not weep over what we can't. There were the usual number of people out of heat in the cold and those with electricity turned off. We do the best we can.

All the things you sent to keep people warm (for people to wear and shoes) were used for the holidays, and some will be given away soon. I have a favor to ask: will you tie your shoes together by the strings or with string. It takes hours to tie shoes and to find mates. We had a young mother who looked almost all day for the mate to blinking tennis shoes for her son. She said he wanted some so bad for Christmas, but the mate was gone. We all looked, and I wanted to go to Wal-Mart and get some, but my gift cards were all gone. You can't make the whole world happy, but, as I tell Daniel, it is wonderful to have that "want too" feeling inside. You make many dreams come true for our people, and I think many times of the old days when I have cried over situations I could do so little about. Like the time a little 6-month-old born to beautiful parents who had nothing but love, and the father was out of work. When the baby died it just about killed all of us, and I knew there was nothing in the family that could take the cost of a funeral. I got together with my sister-in-law – her husband was out of town. She gave me $300, and I got clothes and a cheap casket. I went to the City and asked them to let us have the cheapest lot at the cemetery to bury the six-month-old. They would not let me have a lot on high ground, but they let us have a lot at the back of the new cemetery where the ground was low because the best ground was too expensive. I thought about that water coming in on that beautiful little boy in the cheap casket. When my husband preached the sermon, graveside, and they started to let that little casket down, and the water rushed over it in that hole with only 9 of us standing, I thought my heart would break. I had trouble sleeping for days.

The biggest thing right now is our old 11-year-old truck that is on the blink, and we need it so bad to go get food and donations. We will have to look to Jesus and trust a truck to fall from the sky, like the goat did. I would never have believed a goat would "drop in."

Much love and thanks,

JoAnn Cayce

Conclusion

In October, 2004, Daniel Cayce and his grandmother, JoAnn Cayce, became the first members of the same family to win the National Caring Award. The seventeen-year-old Bearden (Arkansas) high school junior accepted the same award his grandmother had earned in 1992, in Washington, D.C.

At the age of three, Daniel began handing out food during his grandmother's give-aways, and by the time he was 12, he was collecting blankets in the winter and fans in the summer for the needy of South Arkansas. At a recent winter give-away, he distributed 3,000 blankets, 1,500 pots and pans, and 400 sets of dishes.

Last year, he collected and distributed $5,000 worth of school supplies. In 2003, when he discovered that the USDA WIC (Women, Infants, and Children) program excluded baby food, his efforts resulted in delivery of 2,000 pounds of baby food in rural Arkansas. "I believe unless a child has adequate nutrition, he will be left behind in education and in health," Daniel said.

Immediately after returning to the state following acceptance of the Caring Award in Washington, Daniel was told by former Senator David Pryor, dean of the new Clinton School of Public Service that the school had named a new award for him. Flanked by Ted Danson and Mary Steenburgen, the Daniel Cayce Award for Inspirational Leadership in Public Service was unveiled. It will be given each year to a young person who volunteers in the community. Too modest to recount his charity work, it was his mother Joannie who enumerated his many projects.

"I consider (the award) to be more important than an Academy Award — and I have one," said Steenburgen.

Well-rounded and active in Boy Scouts, football, school clubs and his church, Daniel maintains a 4.0 grade point average. He has earned the Governor's Volunteer of Excellence Awards in 2000, 2001, and 2002. He was chosen from among several thousand teens as Arkansas' Teen Volunteer for 2003. For the past two years he has served on an Arkansas Champion Odyssey of the Mind team, which won at all local and state levels, going on to compete in the National and World levels.

Daniel's life took a dramatic turn in late 2002. From December, 2002, to February, 2003, his grandmother suffered four strokes, and he and his mother were running JoAnn Cayce Charity.

Joannie Cayce had Hodgkins Disease in 1981, at which time she was treated with radiation and chemotherapy, all before Daniel was born. Doctors at Houston's M.D. Anderson Cancer Hospital called Daniel's conception and birth a miracle. In May, 2003, as his grandmother recovered, his mother was diagnosed with aggressive breast cancer, and she spent her summer having surgery and chemotherapy.

With these tragedies in his life, Daniel declared that summer S.O.S., the Summer of Success. Along with his other charity work, his letter writing campaign, and speaking opportunities at area churches, food bank distributors and caring organizations, Daniel took on one more project.

When his mother lost all her beautiful red hair from chemotherapy treatments, she was given a pretty wig and three hats. Daniel was upset that the hats were an older style than he wanted for his mom, and he started a project of getting younger-looking hats made. He went to Wal-Mart and bought patterns, tie-dyed and denim material along with Mickey Mouse and camouflage material and took it to an area seamstress. He has accepted donations to help pay for the project and donates all the hats to the Moms with Cancer Center at St. Vincent Hospital in his mother's honor.

Daniel continues to receive awards. With each new challenge he accepts and each added responsibility he takes on, he shows himself to be the hope of the future. Daniel Cayce has the heart, mind and energy to continue the work of his forebears. JoAnn Cayce Charities will continue to be in good hands.

Partial List of JoAnn Cayce's Awards

1988	Woodmen of the World Outstanding Citizen
1989	Arkansas Times Annual Arkansas Heroes Award
1989	President's Volunteer Action Award (George H.W. Bush)
1991	Ladies Home Journal American Heroines
1991	KATV Citizen of the Year
1992	Inducted into Hall of Fame for Caring Americans
1993	Presidential Award (Bill Clinton)
1994	Appreciation Award from SCACAR Board
1995	Award from State of Arkansas (Jim Guy Tucker, Governor)
1997	Governor's Volunteer Excellence Award (Mike Huckabee)
1997	Sister Pierre Voster Outstanding Volunteer Award
1997	Hall of Fame Aging and Adult Services
1998	Ageless Heroes, Blue Cross / Blue Shield
1998	Rotary Paul Harris Fellow Award
1998	Distinguished Service Hunger Coalition
1999	Community of Camden Best Neighbor Award
1999	Community Involvement Award, Blue Cross
2002	Arkansas School Boards Association Award
2003	Prudential Award